'Luan has transformed her years of hard-won experience goldmine of practical, engaging, and no-nonsense advice that every business needs to read before investing another minute in social media. I'm already referring to it regularly at work.'

Will Francis, Digital Marketing Trainer & Speaker

'This book is your roadmap to social media success. A powerful tool for boosting your brand's online impact and a true gem for business growth.'

Dr Leeya Hendricks, Managing Director, Hark Consultants,
Non-Executive Director, Chartered Marketer & Fellow of
the Chartered Institute of Marketing

'In this handy and accessible guide to transforming your business's digital marketing, Luan does not shy away from breaking down the trickier topics. No matter what experience you have in social media, there is something for you in this book!'

Dave Briggs, Founder, Building Brands

'Jam-packed with real-life examples and success stories, *Smart Social Media* offers accessible, practical and invaluable tips on how you can grow your business by elevating your social media presence.'

Lisa Williams, Managing Director, Marketing Donut

'*Smart Social Media* gives you the perfect grounding across all aspects of marketing and branding, and how social media can effectively tie into your strategy to achieve your business goals. Luan leaves no stone unturned to provide you with all the tools you'll need to succeed when using social media in your business. Whether you work alone or in a larger company – if you use social media, you need this book.'

Toby Tetrault, Head of Marketing & Tech, IPSE –
the Association of the Self-Employed

'Yet another book from Luan that is packed with insightful examples and clear explanations. *Smart Social Media* will give you the tools to upgrade your social media strategy and create your foundation for long term success.'

Professor Laura Chamberlain, Professor of Marketing at
Warwick Business School, The University of Warwick

'Two decades on from Facebook's launch and 17 years since the introduction of its ad platform, the opportunities for marketers to make the best of social media still feel unexploited. Familiar platforms evolve and new ones emerge, leaving many brands in need of an up-to-date, simple but comprehensive A–Z guide. I said it often as *Marketing Week* Editor and I say it now: thank heavens for Luan Wise.'

Mark Choueke, Bestselling Author & B2B Marketing Consultant

SMART
SOCIAL MEDIA

How to grow your business
with social media marketing

LUAN WISE

BLOOMSBURY BUSINESS
LONDON · OXFORD · NEW YORK · NEW DELHI · SYDNEY

BLOOMSBURY BUSINESS
Bloomsbury Publishing Plc
50 Bedford Square, London, WC1B 3DP, UK
29 Earlsfort Terrace, Dublin 2, Ireland

First published in Great Britain 2024

A catalogue record for this book is available from the British Library

Library of Congress Cataloging-in-Publication data has been applied for

ISBN: 978-1-3994-1633-7; eBook: 978-1-3994-1634-4

2 4 6 8 10 9 7 5 3 1

Typeset by Deanta Global Publishing Services, Chennai, India
Printed and bound in Great Britain by CPI Group (UK) Ltd, Croydon CR0 4YY

To find out more about our authors and books visit www.bloomsbury.com
and sign up for our newsletters

Contents

Introduction

I'm imagining that you've picked up this book because you want to do more. You're ambitious. You want to grow (and there's many ways to do that). I understand that completely; I consider myself to be a lifelong learner, an avid reader and a constant list writer. Aristotle famously wrote, *'The more you know, the more you realize you don't know.'* When you're a business owner, and a marketer, it feels like the increasing pace of change in the world around you make this an even bigger challenge. I'm not promising all the answers, but I hope by sharing my own learnings, you will not feel so alone. Or overwhelmed. By reading this book, I hope you will feel encouraged and inspired.

When I was approached by the team at Bloomsbury Business to write *Smart Social Media*, I was midway through writing *Planning for Success: A practical guide to setting and achieving your social media marketing goals* (published

'The more you know, the more you realize you don't know'

October 2023), aimed at supporting early career marketers entering the world of work. In collaboration with Warwick Business School, University of Warwick, I carried out quantitative and qualitative research with marketers working in SME businesses in the UK to understand better the industry observations I have built from years of marketing consultancy and delivering social media training. The research findings indicated that a significant proportion of marketers were unsure how best to use social media in a business setting, were unsure how to measure success, and had received little training on using social media in the previous year.

However, new graduates and those in their first marketing role weren't the only ones who were struggling with social media in a business setting. The research indicated that those with several years' experience also experienced a lack of confidence about how to use social media effectively in business, and how to prove its efficacy to the board to secure support and further investment. What persisted was a sense of all parties 'not knowing what they didn't know', and often being misled by vanity metrics and myths of social media as a dark art.

I continue to address those concerns in this book. *Smart Social Media* is aimed at individuals who are responsible for social media marketing in their business, and who find themselves asking what they might be missing. What more could they be doing? How could they be using metrics more effectively? How could they best partner with influencers to grow the business? It is for those who are both involved in strategic planning as well as the tactical implementation of social media marketing.

If you are reading this book, I assume you are familiar with using social media and the language associated with it. It is not a media channel you can expect to use successfully if you are not part of the ecosystem, watching and learning from your own personal experiences.

The terms customers, consumers, target audience and prospects may be used interchangeably to refer to individuals or groups engaging with the purchase of products or services.

Throughout the book, I have used the term 'business'. I believe the content of the book is applicable to both B2C

(Business-to-Consumer) and B2B (Business-to-Business) contexts, and also for those working in not-for-profit organizations or educational institutions. It may also be used interchangeably with 'brand' when discussing businesses with diverse activities and product lines. I have tried to use varied examples and case studies throughout, and to share evergreen principles to guide and inform how you use social media, whatever sector you are working in, and however much the platforms themselves change.

As we witness the integration of artificial intelligence (AI), augmented reality (AR), and virtual reality (VR) into social media platforms, I believe the future of social media marketing holds even more exciting opportunities for businesses. Those willing to embrace innovation and adapt to the dynamic shifts in consumer behaviours and emerging trends can achieve sustainable growth, whether that's through market or product development, operational efficiencies, physical presence (locations) and employee headcounts or other relevant criteria.

Are you ready? Let's get started...

Chapter 1

Principles for effective social media marketing

Effective social media marketing relies on several key principles; including understanding the target audience, consistency and data insights.

- Knowing who you are communicating with requires an understanding of demographics, psychographics and behaviours. This level of insight guides platform selection, content creation and the brand experience to achieve authentic reception and engagement.
- Establishing a consistent identity across social media platforms, and regular cadence of posting builds awareness and front-of-mind recall. High-quality content fosters trust and loyalty. As we will discover, social media marketing can support all stages of the marketing funnel and areas of a business (not just marketing).
- Tracking and analysing social media metrics is fundamental for optimization. By setting clear goals and objectives that align with the business strategy, performance can be measured. Activities that are working well can be

repeated and amplified, and other activities can be adjusted accordingly.

This might sound simple but social media changes daily. While various platforms and tools are readily available to support our businesses, much is beyond our control in terms of the changes platforms might make to features and the algorithms being used. We need to plan and work around this. We need to continually review and adapt; to test and learn. Social media users are also susceptible to changes happening in their own lives, and the world around them – from key events to cultural trends.

Change presents both challenges and opportunities. By understanding change and applying our core principles, we *can* reap the rewards, minimize the risks, and successfully grow our businesses.

We *can* reap the rewards, minimize the risks, and successfully grow our businesses

The evolution of marketing

The term 'marketing', a derivation of the Latin word *mercatus* meaning marketplace or merchant, first appeared in the sixteenth century, when it referred to the process of buying and selling at a market. At that time, marketing was typically a local affair, with customers buying from, and selling to, people who likely lived close to them and with whom they were familiar. By the nineteenth century, the term 'marketing' had evolved to describe the commercial activities that assist in the buying and selling of products and services: a shift from the transaction itself to the activities that support and encourage that transaction. This definition is closer to what we understand today by marketing.

The rise of industrialization, the development of better transport links, and the introduction of the postal service meant that by the nineteenth century, marketing could expand much wider than the local sphere, and businesses began to produce product variations to appeal to the needs of different groups of customers.

Jump to the present day, and the current definition from the American Marketing Association is *'Marketing is the activity, set of institutions, and processes for creating, communicating, delivering, and exchanging offerings that have value for customers, clients, partners, and society at large.'* Marketing, therefore, is no longer solely about buying and selling or the activities that support them, but a series of actions from identifying a need for a product – or service – to its development, the range of ways in which potential customers are made aware of its existence.

From the early 1990s, the development of the Internet and other technologies, from personal computers to smartphones, has changed the way we live and work, and inevitably it has changed the role and activities of marketing. Customers are no longer restricted to buying from the local market, from people who are their neighbours, nor are businesses compelled to transact face to face. Technology means we can communicate with customers wherever they are in the world, and at any time of the day.

Traditional marketing communications relied heavily on newspapers, televisions, radio and direct mail as primary channels for promotion. These methods have not disappeared; instead, they have evolved to become integral components of a broader marketing toolkit, alongside new online opportunities.

Those born since the late 1990s have not known life without either the Internet or social media. As the nature of the World

Wide Web developed, Web 2.0 became more participatory, with users able to interact and collaborate with each other (Web 1.0 was limited to viewing content in a passive manner). Now, Web 3.0 is emerging as the next phase of the internet, focused on giving users more control over their data and online interactions through decentralization and new technologies like blockchain.

Since the early days of social media – an umbrella term that defines the various activities that integrate technology, social interaction and the construction of words, video and audio – its use and reach has grown exponentially. Nor is it the preserve of the digital native – social media is used by every generation. A quick look at the development of social media will illustrate how it has come to be a part of our everyday lives.

One of the pioneering social media platforms was Six Degrees, founded in 1997, which allowed users to create profiles and connect with each other. In the early 2000s, platforms such as Friendster, Myspace and LinkedIn followed suit, each catering to specific aspects of social networking. Although Friendster and Myspace have now disappeared, LinkedIn – the B2B social networking site – continues to grow.

The launch of Facebook in 2004 marked a significant turning point for social media, revolutionizing the ways in which people connect, share information and engage online. Originally designed for US college students, it soon expanded to allow everyone (anywhere) to connect with friends and family members.

Facebook Pages were among the first tools created specifically for businesses to establish their presence on social media; indeed Facebook was the first social media platform to introduce advertising in 2007. At the time, Facebook founder and CEO Mark Zuckerberg said, 'Facebook Ads represent a completely new way of advertising online. For the last hundred years, media has been pushed out to people, but now marketers are going to be a part of the conversation.' Social media wasn't just changing our personal interactions; it was changing the opportunities for marketing too.

Twitter (now X) launched in 2006, pioneered the concept of microblogging by enabling users to share thoughts, updates and news in a concise way. In 2010, Instagram was born, focusing on visual content and aesthetics. Sensing the growing popularity of this new platform, it was acquired by Facebook in 2012 and is now part of the Meta family of apps. Snapchat, launched in 2011, introduced ephemeral content, allowing users to share moments that disappeared after a set time. The meteoric rise of TikTok in 2020 ushered in a whole new era of video marketing, with other platforms adding similar features – for example, Reels on Facebook and Instagram and Shorts on YouTube.

Social media has wholly transformed the marketing landscape. In January 2024, 5.35 billion (66.2 per cent) of the global population use the Internet, and 5.04 billion (62.3 per cent) are active users of social media,

Social media has wholly transformed the marketing landscape

spending an average 2 hours 23 minutes a day across 6.7 different platforms. Compare this to an average daily consumption of 1 hour 41 minutes a day reading press media (online and physical print), 50 minutes listening to broadcast radio, and 3 hours 6 minutes of television viewing time (broadcast and streaming). (Source: DataReportal).

However, it's important to remember that no channel works in isolation. As consumers we not only access multiple social media platforms, but we also see marketing messages in more than one place, across different media. Here's a great example provided by Royal Mail's MarketReach team where social media is used to amplify the messaging from traditional media (direct mail).

Case study: The National Trust

The National Trust in the UK wanted to address the challenge of getting kids out of their bedrooms, away from their computers and into the countryside with a creative solution: a magic poster promoting outdoor adventures.

Recognizing that children's suggestions often lead to the best activities, they launched the '50 Things to do before you're 11¾' campaign to reintroduce families to nature-based adventures. Targeting parents of children aged 5 to 11¾, they crafted a night-time walk poster for children's bedrooms. This magic poster featured a hidden night-time scene, revealed by phosphorescent ink, captivating kids and inspiring them to explore outdoors.

The results were impressive, with the magic Night Safari poster driving engagement, app downloads and social mentions. The campaign saw a huge increase in discussion, with social mentions doubling; as one mum tweeted, 'Loving the glow in the dark poster…it's been quite a talking point at bedtime.'

Most importantly, the campaign led to happier, healthier children spending more time outdoors. Over 90,000 children signed up for the '50 Things' campaign, collectively spending 23 extra years playing outside.

The importance of market orientation

Throughout the evolution of business philosophies, there has been a transformative journey from a production orientation to a selling orientation and ultimately to a marketing orientation. In the early stages, businesses were primarily concerned with efficient production and meeting market demands. However, as markets grew more competitive, a selling orientation emerged, emphasizing the need to actively persuade customers to choose existing products. The pivotal shift towards a marketing orientation, from the 1950s onwards, signifies a modern perspective where businesses prioritize a comprehensive understanding of customer needs and desires. This approach involves meticulous market research, customer-centric product development, and the cultivation of long-term relationships.

Market orientation places the customer at the forefront of decision-making. By actively seeking to understand and meet customer needs, business can adapt to changing market dynamics and innovate effectively. **Social media is about people** This customer-centric approach not only enhances customer satisfaction and loyalty, but also provides businesses with a competitive advantage to stand out from the crowd.

Ironically, although social media is predicated on the development of technology, as Brian Solis, the American futurist observes, 'Social media is about sociology and psychology more than technology.' Social media is about people. Understanding how people think, feel and act has become critical for businesses seeking to grow. This starts with understanding how customers make decisions to purchase.

The decision-making process is a journey we all go on when considering a product or service. From a marketing perspective we can use the AIDA model to explain it.

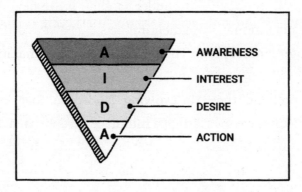

FIGURE 1.1 THE AIDA MODEL

Developed by American advertising strategist Elias St Elmo Lewis in 1898 as a multi-stage model for sales, the AIDA model, pictured in Figure 1.1 above, highlights the buying decision process that begins with capturing attention, prompting potential customers to take notice, and become aware of the offering (A = Awareness). Subsequently, we move to generate a deeper level of interest (I) which can be supported by providing information that sustains a potential customer's curiosity. As the process continues, a sense of desire (D) is stimulated by an emotional connection or understanding of the product/service's value. Finally, the journey concludes with a taking of action (A), most likely a purchase. After purchase, a customer may become loyal and make repeat purchases. For low

The role of marketing is to influence decision-making

value, everyday products such as food and drink, this decision-making process is relatively short. For large value purchases such as a family car, holiday or – at work – the purchase of new software or capital equipment, the process can take much longer. It can also include more than one person.

Decision-making is influenced by internal factors including personal preferences, attitudes, motivations and perceptions, while external factors encompass cultural, social, economic and environmental influences. By understanding these factors – both emotional and rational – and their impacts, businesses can navigate the intricate landscape of behavioural decision-making more effectively.

To comprehend the ever-evolving landscape that influences decision-making, we must adopt a multifaceted approach. First and foremost, staying abreast of market trends and industry insights is essential. This is relatively easy to do with the plethora of news sources and alerts available. To dive deeper involves continuous research and analysis, utilizing tools such as market studies and customer surveys. Collaborating with cross-functional teams and fostering a culture of innovation within the business encourages diverse perspectives, ensuring a comprehensive understanding of the changing world around us. The information needs to be captured and referred to regularly. Traditional models such as PESTLE and SWOT provide useful frameworks for capturing and analysing environmental factors. You can learn about these frameworks in Appendix 1 and 2.

Ultimately, the role of marketing is to influence decision-making and change behaviours. Let's take a look at a case study for two Unilever brands.

Case study: The role of social media in encouraging sustainable choices

A 2023 study commissioned by two Unilever brands (Dove and Hellmann's), and conducted by the Behavioural Insights

Team with a group of nine influential creators from TikTok and Instagram, found that social media ranks as one of the most influential sources of sustainability information, and that influencer content can make people change their behaviour for the better. For the study, 30 pieces of social content about sustainability (encouraging people to waste less food and use less plastic) were tested to measure their impact on consumers. The study involved 6,000 participants across the UK, US and Canada.

- 75 per cent of people surveyed said that the content made them more likely to adopt sustainable behaviours.
- 78 per cent of people surveyed said social media is the information source most likely to encourage them to act more sustainably, ahead of TV documentaries (48 per cent), news articles (38 per cent) and government campaigns (20 per cent).
- 83 per cent of people surveyed think TikTok and Instagram are good places to get advice about how to live sustainably.

Understanding influence

Influence means the capacity to have an effect on the character, development or behaviour of someone or something. We all

We all experience influence

experience influence, whether it be consciously or unconsciously. Who have you spoken to today? What have you read, watched or listened to? Have those interactions shaped your thoughts, decisions and behaviours in any way?

Sometimes the influence can manifest with immediate effects, while at other times, its impact unfolds gradually over the long term. For marketing, this underscores the importance of multiple touchpoints throughout the decision-making journey as sustained interactions and consistent messaging contribute to building lasting connections and impacts. We also need to be aware of external influences that might guide our audiences in other directions (for example, competitors).

Influence: The Psychology of Persuasion by Robert Cialdini is a seminal work that explores the science of persuasion and the factors that drive people to say 'yes'. The book introduces six fundamental principles of persuasion, each of which holds significant relevance for social media marketing.

Cialdini's first principle, **reciprocity**, highlights the effectiveness of giving before expecting to receive. In the context of social media marketing, businesses often initiate this principle by offering valuable content, such as informative blog posts, webinars or downloadable resources, to their audience. By providing something of value upfront, businesses create a sense of goodwill and reciprocity. This encourages users to engage with the brand, share its content or even make purchases.

The second principle, **social proof**, underscores the human tendency to follow the actions of others. Social media marketing leverages this principle by showcasing engagement metrics (i.e. likes, comments and shares) along with user-generated content to demonstrate a brand's popularity and trustworthiness. These visible indicators tap into the psychological need for conformity and belonging, reinforcing the credibility and appeal of the brand.

Urgency is the third principle. It triggers a sense of FOMO (Fear of Missing Out) in users. Businesses often employ tactics such as time-related offers, early booking discounts and limited availability to motivate users to take immediate action, aligning with the principles of social proof and scarcity.

Cialdini's fourth principle, **authority**, emphasizes the influence of expertise and credibility. Businesses and individuals can establish authority by sharing content that demonstrates their industry knowledge and expertise. Articles, whitepapers or videos providing valuable insights convey not only added value but also authority in the field.

Cialdini's principle of **liking** suggests that people are more likely to say 'yes' to those they know and like.

Social media content that is relatable and authentic helps audiences get to know and like each other. By building genuine connections and fostering positive sentiment, businesses and individuals cultivate liking among their audience.

The final principle, **scarcity**, revolves around the creation of a sense of rarity or exclusivity. By strategically using scarcity, businesses not only stimulate immediate engagement but also enhance the perceived value of their offerings, making them even more enticing to their target audience.

These principles will be important to remember when you get to Chapter 5, 'Guiding the buyer's journey with social media content'.

Effective marketing

Effective marketing hinges on the key principles we have mentioned so far – namely, understanding audiences and their behaviours; consistency in communicating with our audiences; and utilizing analytics to assess performance.

But what do we mean by 'effective' marketing? To be effective, we are accomplishing a purpose, and producing an intended or expected result. We need to be completely clear on the results we wish to achieve. We need to provide those viewing our social media content with clear next steps or calls-to-action (CTA). Our purpose is our starting point, **Understanding, and alignment, are critical to achieving success** and provides guiding points of reference for day-to-day tactical implementation, as well as being crucial for strategic-level reporting.

Take some time to ensure that you have a clear understanding of what you wish to achieve for your business. You might continue reading and then come back to this task, but please do not dive into social media marketing without knowing exactly what you wish to achieve. The research underpinning my book *Planning for Success: A practical guide to setting and achieving your social media marketing goals* highlighted that just under half of the marketers we surveyed did not understand, or were unsure, how social media fitted into their business plan, or how to set the right objectives. This understanding, and alignment, are critical to achieving success.

Once your purpose is clear and objectives are defined, effectiveness can be assessed via key performance indicators (KPIs). For social media marketing, here are some common measures:

- **Reach and impressions:** Reach represents the total number of unique users who have seen a particular social media post, while impressions measure the total number of times a post has been displayed. These metrics provide insights into the content's visibility and potential exposure to target audiences.

- **Engagement rate:** Engagement rate calculates the level of interaction with the content posted on social media by expressing engagements such as likes, comments, shares and clicks as a percentage against follower numbers or impressions. A higher engagement rate suggests that the content is resonating with the audience.
- **Follower growth:** This KPI measures the increase in the number of followers on social media platforms over a specific period. It indicates whether you are successfully building your online audience.
- **Click through rate (CTR):** CTR measures the percentage of users who click on a link included in a social media post or ad. It plays a role in evaluating the effectiveness of calls-to-action (CTA).
- **Website traffic:** This KPI identifies website traffic that originates from social media platforms. It helps in understanding the role of social media in driving website visits and subsequent actions (conversions) such as time on page reading a blog, downloading a PDF document or making a purchase.
- **Conversion rate:** Conversion rate tracks the percentage of social media users who take the desired call-to-action.
- **Cost per acquisition (CPA):** CPA measures the cost of acquiring a new customer through social media marketing efforts. It's particularly important for evaluating the cost-effectiveness of advertising campaigns.
- **Customer lifetime value (CLV):** CLV estimates the total value a customer is expected to bring to the business over their entire relationship. It helps in understanding the

long-term impact of social media marketing efforts on customer retention and revenue.

- **Share of voice (SOV):** This KPI assesses a brand's presence in comparison to its competitors on social media platforms. It helps gauge the brand's share of the overall online conversation in its industry.
- **Sentiment:** Sentiment analysis involves tracking and analysing mentions of a brand on social media to determine whether the sentiment is positive, negative or neutral. It helps in understanding perception and managing reputation.

For an up-to-date guide to social media analytics and KPIs visit www.luanwise.co.uk/books/smart-social-media or scan the QR code below.

Measuring the effectiveness of social media efforts is crucial for any business, yet it poses challenges due to the complexity of attributing success to individual posts or metrics. This complexity arises from the multifaceted nature of social media, where interactions occur across various platforms and content types. To overcome this challenge, businesses should develop a dashboard that aligns KPIs with the overarching business goals. With regular reviews this will guide decision-making and future activities.

Chapter summary

The evolution of marketing has been fuelled by technology, enabling brands to expand, reach and nurture meaningful connections with customers across digital platforms. However, while new tools and channels continue to emerge, success still lies in understanding human behaviour and the decision-making process.

As this chapter outlines, adopting a marketing orientation that prioritizes customers is key for growth. Businesses must invest time researching target audiences and analysing data. With people spending over two hours on social media daily, platforms such as Facebook, X (Twitter) and LinkedIn present valuable opportunities to cost-effectively influence and interact with existing and potential customers. Yet cutting through the noise requires grasping the psychology that compels engagement. Cialdini's six principles of persuasion provide a blueprint for creating content and campaigns optimized for response.

While authenticity builds authority and community fuels advocacy, measurement is equally vital for growth. Tightly aligning activities with business goals and tracking performance through defined KPIs allows for continual optimization in an ever-changing landscape.

Chapter 2

Getting to know your customers

In the words of American poet and civil rights activist Maya Angelou, *'I've learned that people will forget what you said, people will forget what you did, but people will never forget how you made them feel.'* This timeless wisdom resonates with an undeniable truth in the world of social media marketing – how you and your products/ services make your customers feel is at the heart of your success.

But first, your customers need to know who you are, what you do, and what your business stands for. Second, you need to get to know your customers. You could argue that this should be the other way round. **Your customers need to know who you are** You need to get to know your customers before they can get to know you. In an ideal world, it's a two-way process that happens simultaneously.

As we will discover in Chapter 4, building a robust online presence involves crafting a clear and compelling brand identity. This extends beyond a logo or tagline; it encompasses the values, mission and unique qualities that set your business apart from others. It's essential to have a deep understanding of how your product or service addresses the needs and pain points of your customers so you can be recognized as the solution provider.

In the ever-changing world of modern business, it's vital for a business to find a lasting place in the minds of its intended audience. This recognition isn't just a strategic advantage: it's a driver for long-term growth and sustainability. There is no point in being the best in your industry if no one knows about you or your products/ services and the problems you can solve for them.

Front of mind positioning

In the book, *Positioning: The Battle for Your Mind*, Al Ries and Jack Trout highlight the importance of how a brand is perceived in the mind of the customer.

Positioning, as described by Ries and Trout, is about occupying a distinct and memorable place in the minds of consumers. It's the mental real estate that a brand holds in the consciousness of its target audience. When a business is known and recognized by its target audience, it secures a prominent place in their mental landscape. This 'front of mind' awareness makes the business the first choice when consumers have relevant needs or preferences, which is a significant advantage in a crowded market. It's akin to being the default option when a consumer thinks about a particular product or service category. It ensures that your brand is the go-to choice, providing an edge over competitors and fostering brand loyalty. This applies to both individuals, in terms of personal brands, and businesses.

Let's try it. What business comes to mind when you think of a laptop computer? How about where to buy books? Who comes to mind when you go in search of a podcast to listen to?

As the examples above show, positioning effectively reduces the size of the market, as when people think about the product or service they require, often only one name comes to mind.

The next step is to ensure that the response is not only immediate, but also favourable. This involves cultivating positive associations with the brand, whether through quality, reliability, innovation or other distinguishing factors.

Return your thoughts to the laptop computer, bookstore and podcast. Would you be happy to purchase from the businesses that came to mind first? Would you take advice from the podcast host? Or is there something that might make you consider an alternative brand?

Understanding customer needs

To truly connect and engage with your audience, you must understand them intimately. It's not enough to simply broadcast your message to your audience, and hope that it will be received and understood. Every social media user is inundated with an overwhelming amount of information daily. To stand out amidst this digital clutter, capture attention and stop the scroll, social media content needs to resonate with the specific needs of your target audience. The way to ensure this is by conducting research so you know exactly what your prospective customers want and need.

Case study: Netflix

Customer research plays a critical role in shaping successful businesses. An excellent example of this in practice is the transformation of Netflix. In the early 2000s, Netflix primarily operated as a DVD rental service, and has since evolved into a global streaming platform. Netflix recognized the value of delving deep into their users' viewing habits and preferences. By conducting thorough customer research, they began offering personalized content recommendations. This emotionally resonant approach made users feel understood and valued, fostering a stronger connection to the platform. To enable global expansion, Netflix used customer research to understand cultural differences and the diverse emotional ties and viewing habits inherent in different international markets.

Netflix continually refine their user interface and experiences based on research. For example, noticing the significant shift in customer behaviour towards 'binge-watching' supported their move into original content production with House of Cards in 2013. Netflix continues to create a diverse array of award-winning series, films and documentaries, including *Stranger Things*, *The Crown* and *The Queen's Gambit*, all contributing to the platform's global success and cultural impact. In January 2024, Netflix reported over 260 million paid memberships in over 190 countries.

By contrast, Blockbuster, once a dominant player in the video and DVD rental industry, failed to understand and adapt to changing customer behaviours. The company's inability to pivot ultimately led to their bankruptcy, while Netflix's customer-centric approach has allowed them to survive and thrive.

For further information on Netflix, I recommend reading *That Will Never Work: The Birth of Netflix* by the first CEO and co-founder, Marc Randolph.

Creating a customer persona

A customer persona, also known as a buyer persona or ideal customer portrait, is a reflection of your ideal target customer based on research and data. It is a detailed profile that includes demographic information, motivations, preferences and behaviours. By creating customer personas, you can make informed decisions about activities within your business, including social media marketing and the platforms you will use, based on a deep understanding of target audience characteristics and desires.

Personas bring to life desk-research and data points to a human level where you can see audiences as living, breathing individuals with dreams, aspirations and needs for your products or services. Knowing and serving your customers is the key to growth and success in the world of marketing as it makes your messages more focused and pertinent. It's often said in marketing that if you try to market to everyone you end up marketing to no one. Personas help you to craft messages that resonate deeply with your target audience and help them to feel that you and your business understand their problems and needs.

If you try to market to everyone you end up marketing to no one

If you have not yet created customer personas, please stop here. These are an essential foundation for your growth journey and require careful consideration and preparation. Please refer to Appendix 3 for persona resources.

Case study: Apple Inc

Few companies exemplify the power of knowing their customers better than Apple Inc.

Founder Steve Jobs famously did not believe in traditional market research methodologies, often stating that customers didn't know what they wanted until Apple showed it to them.

Instead, he relied on his intuition and a deep understanding of design and technology to create products that would resonate with customers on an emotional level.

Apple's products, such as the iPhone, iPad and MacBook, are designed with a deep understanding of user behaviour and preferences. Their sleek designs, user-friendly interfaces, and integration across the Apple ecosystem reflect this insight.

Apple's marketing campaigns resonate with emotions and aspirations. They don't merely sell products; they sell experiences and lifestyles. The 'Think Different' campaign launched in 1997 was a revolutionary initiative that urged customers to embrace innovation and individuality. The evergreen 'Shot on iPhone' campaign, which showcases user-generated content, not only highlights the product's camera capabilities but also celebrates the creativity and passion of Apple users.

The Apple Store, both physical and online, is designed to provide a seamless and personalized customer experience. Apple's support and customer service are also legendary, creating trust and loyalty among its customers.

Without a doubt, Apple's success lies in its continuous effort to know its customers intimately, predict their needs, and exceed their expectations.

The 'know, like, trust' factor

The 'know, like, trust' factor emphasizes the importance of building relationships with potential customers. The idea is that people are more likely to do business with someone they know, like and trust than with someone they don't. To build trust with potential customers, businesses and individuals must first make themselves known and likable.

The 'know' stage is about making potential customers aware of your brand and what you have to offer. This can be done through various marketing channels, including social media. Social media platforms like Facebook, Instagram and LinkedIn allow businesses to reach a large audience and share information about their products and services. By consistently posting engaging content, businesses can increase their visibility and make themselves known to potential customers. This is increasingly important as user behaviours are shifting from discovering brands via search engines to discovery via social media search.

The 'like' stage is about creating a connection with potential customers. This can be done by sharing personal stories, highlighting the people behind the brand, and engaging with followers on social media. By showing their human side, businesses can make themselves more relatable and likable to potential customers. There is an interplay between individuals and brands emerging in terms of branding, but don't worry, it's not essential – brands can successfully develop their identities in a personable style without relying on individuals. Take a look at some of the social media accounts of brands such as Aldi, Monzo and Mailchimp for examples.

Finally, the 'trust' stage is about establishing credibility and reliability with potential customers. This can be done by sharing customer testimonials, reviews and case studies. By demonstrating that other people have had positive experiences with your brand, businesses can build trust with potential customers and increase their likelihood of making a purchase.

Social media is a linchpin in each phase of the 'know, like, trust' factor. By consistently posting engaging content, responding to comments and messages, and sharing social proof, businesses and individuals can build and nurture relationships with potential customers and increase their chances of making a sale, or receiving referrals. Additionally, social media provides an opportunity to showcase their brand personality and values, which can make them more relatable and likable to potential customers.

Trust is the currency of the digital realm

When you demonstrate a deep understanding of your customers' needs and consistently deliver on your promises, you build a reputation as a trustworthy and reliable brand. Trust is the currency of the digital realm, and businesses that can earn it will thrive.

Understanding rational and emotional customer needs

Understanding the role of rational and emotional needs is also paramount for businesses striving to forge genuine connections with their customers.

Rational needs, often associated with logic and practicality, drive customers and businesses to make informed decisions based on tangible factors. These needs often revolve around the functional aspects of a product or service, addressing questions like, 'Does this solution meet my specific problem or requirement?' Rational needs can be quantifiable and objective, with customers seeking attributes such as affordability, reliability and efficiency. It is vital for businesses to recognize that while rational needs provide a foundation for the decision-making process, they alone seldom evoke brand loyalty or customer advocacy.

Contrastingly, emotional needs delve into the deeper, often subconscious desires and aspirations of individuals. These needs are subjective, rooted in feelings, and are intricately tied to the human experience. Author of *Lovemarks: The future beyond brands*, Kevin Roberts has stated that the buying decision is 80 per cent emotional. Emotional needs encompass a spectrum of desires, such as the longing for belonging, the pursuit of happiness, the yearning for recognition, and the thirst for self-fulfilment. Emotions drive buying behaviours. Marketing that taps into emotions creates connections that go far beyond rationality.

Case study: New Coke

As we saw at the start of the chapter, what people remember most is how we make them feel.

However, misjudging deep emotional connections can cause significant problems for a business. You might recall the story of 'New Coke', introduced by The Coca-Cola Company in 1985. Despite positive taste test results, Coca-Cola overlooked the emotional connection customers had with the original brand's heritage and tradition. This emotional attachment triggered a massive consumer backlash, leading to the reintroduction of the classic formula as 'Coca-Cola Classic' within just three months.

There is a common perception that B2C (Business-to-Consumer) marketing tends to be more emotional, while B2B (Business-to-Business) marketing is more rational. This oversimplification can be misleading. In reality, both B2C and B2B marketing involve a complex mix of rational and emotional factors.

B2C marketing may seem more emotional because it often directly targets individual customers, playing on their personal desires, preferences and emotions. However, even in B2C scenarios, rational considerations like product specifications, pricing and convenience play a significant role in the decision-making process. In B2B marketing, emotional elements still come into play, as individuals within those businesses are involved in making decisions over what and when to buy. Although an individual is not spending their own money, people don't want to make a bad decision that could upset colleagues and potentially put their job at risk. It's why

Rational and emotional needs are not mutually exclusive

the classic quote 'you won't get fired for buying IBM' is often cited.

It's important to recognize that rational and emotional needs are not mutually exclusive. They often intersect and interact throughout the buying decision process.

Suppose a B2B company is considering a technology hardware upgrade, such as replacing its aging servers. The company focuses on factors like performance, scalability, cost-effectiveness and technical specifications when evaluating server options. The decision-makers might feel a sense of excitement about the potential for improved efficiency and a more advanced tech environment. They may also experience a sense of relief, knowing they are investing in the future success of the business. In this case, the rational needs drive the technical evaluation, while the emotional needs provide motivation and enthusiasm for the change.

In a B2C context, a family is looking to buy a new car. The family will consider factors like safety features, seating capacity, fuel efficiency and overall cost. The parents may feel a sense of security knowing their family is safe in the vehicle, while the children might experience excitement about road trips and family adventures in the new car. In this example, the rational needs help select a car that meets practical requirements, while the emotional needs build an emotional connection to the vehicle and the experiences it will enable.

- In a rational-only message for a car, a marketing campaign might emphasize specific features such as fuel efficiency, high safety ratings and advanced technology like lane-keeping assist and adaptive cruise control. The appeal here is purely practical, targeting customers who prioritize logical considerations when making a purchasing decision.
- Conversely, an emotional-only message could focus on the joy of driving and the emotional satisfaction derived from the car's design. For instance, the campaign might depict scenes of carefree road trips, the wind in the hair, and the emotional fulfilment associated with owning a stylish and aesthetically pleasing vehicle. This approach aims to evoke feelings of excitement, freedom and pride in ownership.
- In a message that encompasses both rational and emotional needs, the marketing materials could showcase the car's advanced safety features, emphasizing the peace of mind that comes with features like collision avoidance systems. Simultaneously, the campaign could highlight the thrill of the driving experience, weaving narratives around the sense of adventure and the emotional connection someone forms with the vehicle. By integrating both practical and emotional aspects, this approach aims to appeal to a broader audience, acknowledging the rational concerns while creating a more profound and well-rounded connection with the customer.

The key to successful marketing, in both B2C and B2B environments, lies in recognizing the nuanced blend of rational and emotional factors that influence consumer behaviour and the need to connect with both the head and the heart. Once again, research will help you to understand how rational and emotional factors come into play for your target customers.

Emotions and consumer behaviour

In The New Science of Customer Emotions (*Harvard Business Review*, 2015), Scott Magids, Alan Zorfas and Daniel Leemon identified 300 universal motivating emotions and measured their impact on consumer behaviour.

Magids et al. consider customers to be emotionally connected to a brand when it aligns with their motivations and helps them fulfil deep, often unconscious, desires. Examples of important emotional motivators include desires to 'stand out from the crowd', 'have confidence in the future' and 'enjoy a sense of wellbeing'. They discovered that although brands might be liked or trusted, most fail to align themselves with the emotions that drive their customers' most profitable behaviours. They found that customers become more valuable at each step of a predictable 'emotional connection pathway' as they transition from (1) being unconnected to (2) being highly satisfied to (3) perceiving brand differentiation to (4) being fully connected.

'The pathway is an important guide to where companies should invest—and it reveals that they often invest in the wrong places. To increase revenue and market share, many companies focus on turning dissatisfied customers into satisfied ones. However, our analysis

shows that moving customers from highly satisfied to fully connected can have three times the return of moving them from unconnected to highly satisfied. And the highest returns we've seen have come from focusing on customers who are already fully connected to the category—from maximizing their value and attracting more of them to your brand.'

Do you know what the emotional connectors are between your business and your customers?

Can you develop your growth strategy based on increasing emotional connection?

Social media and emotional connection

Social media plays a pivotal role in fostering emotional connections between individuals and businesses. It provides a direct and interactive platform to engage with audiences, listen to their feedback, and respond to their needs and concerns. Through carefully crafted content and authentic storytelling businesses can establish a sense of authenticity and transparency, which resonates with customers on a deeper emotional level.

A sense of trust and empathy can be created by sharing relatable and humanizing content, showcasing the business's values, and even acknowledging and addressing issues publicly. Moreover, the ability to connect with like-minded individuals through social media platforms further enhances the emotional bond between individuals and businesses, ultimately leading to increased brand loyalty and advocacy.

As we saw earlier, when Coca-Cola overlooked its customers' attachment to the original formulation of the drink, sales fell.

One of the most successful techniques for creating emotional attachment and influencing preferences for brands is by connecting people to previous experiences. Nostalgia, for example, can be a powerful emotional driver when it comes to buying decisions, as the following case study from LEGO demonstrates.

Case study: LEGO

For over 90 years, LEGO has captivated the hearts and minds of both young and old, becoming a household name and an iconic symbol of play and construction around the world.

LEGO has consistently embraced nostalgia as a core component of its social media marketing content. The brand's ability to tap into the sentimental value associated with its iconic plastic bricks has been instrumental in not only strengthening its connection with existing fans but also attracting new generations of builders and enthusiasts.

LEGO frequently revisits and re-releases classic sets that evoke nostalgia among adult fans who grew up playing with them. The brand's social media channels showcase these re-releases, celebrating the heritage of the products. This content not only drives sales among adult collectors but also generates significant buzz and conversation on social media platforms so that fans can be a part of the ongoing success story of the LEGO brand.

How might you tap into nostalgia/previous positive experiences to build an emotional connection with your target audience? Can you create campaigns that revisit and celebrate past successes, or highlight the evolution of your product perhaps?

In *Using Behavioural Science in Marketing*, author Nancy Harhut offers the following list of 'Smart ways to inject emotion into your marketing message':

- Prompt your prospect to imagine how good it will feel to save time and personal effort by using your product or service.
- Use pictures and colours to elicit an emotional response.
- Point out the painful situation your target can avoid by adopting your product.
- Make your customer feel special or superior because they use your product.
- Proactively help your prospect before asking them to buy.
- Emphasize that your prospect will be making a popular choice that no one will blame them for.
- Tell the story of how someone became a workplace hero thanks to your product or service.
- Focus on the experience of owning or using your product, along with its features and benefits.

So far, we have looked at how we might use social media to communicate with our target customers. Now it's time to consider what happens when they communicate with us. **Communication, after all, is a two-way process** and if we know how to listen and respond appropriately, customer communications can be a valuable source of business information. Let's begin by considering customer care.

The importance of customer care on social media

Communication between individuals and businesses via social media is often instigated by a customer care-related issue, such as a question about products/services or airing a complaint. In the past, many customers turned to social media as a channel of escalation when more traditional service channels failed to address their concerns. Today's customers are increasingly using social media for general requests, queries and feedback – even compliments.

Leigh Hopwood, CEO of the Call Centre Management Association (CCMA), comments: *'Many of our members are geared up to handle customer contact via social media. With some customers opting to use Facebook and X (Twitter) over voice and email; it has become a valuable channel for quick synchronous interactions.'*

Unsurprisingly, individuals have expectations when they communicate with a business on social media, whether it's via a public post or private message, to receive a response. According to research by Khoros (May 2023), half of social media users expect a brand to respond to their message or post about a complaint within three hours. The problem does not necessarily have to be resolved within this three-hour window, but timeliness is the first stage in the process of a positive conversation.

Providing customer care on social media provides a more favourable view of brands. The Khoros research also highlighted that when consumers' timeframes for receiving a response to messages and posts involving complaints are met, they are more likely to continue giving business to the brand, become more receptive to a brand's advertisements, encourage friends and family to buy a brand's products or use their service, and will praise or recommend the brand on their own social media accounts. Conversely, not responding to customer care messages or taking too long to reply to an initial request can have repercussions with individuals making their complaints public, both online and offline, and they are likely to stop giving their business to the brand.

According to Salesforce's 'State of the Connected Customer' report, factors like cost-of-living and technological advancement are leading people to rethink what's important, including where and how they spend their money. Eighty per cent of customers say the experience a company provides is as important as its products and services.

Social media customer care does not have to be arduous: it can be as simple as responding to public posts or private messages; however, many businesses use social media for social listening to find brand mentions. This can be to resolve questions, address concerns and to acknowledge and thank individuals for positive shout-outs, ensuring that conversations are not just reactive, but also proactive and most importantly 'social'!

Choosing the right social media platforms for your business

Choosing the right social media platforms for your business is a pivotal decision that requires careful consideration of various factors. In my book *Planning for Success*, I outlined a series of questions to guide the process of selecting the most suitable platforms based on your goals, target audience, competitor analysis and available resources.

Set clear goals and objectives:
Before diving into platform selection, it's essential to establish clear social media goals and objectives that align with your overall business plan. Are you aiming to increase brand awareness, drive website traffic, generate leads or boost sales?

Know your audience:
Understanding your target audience is fundamental in determining which platforms to prioritize. Utilize customer personas and market research to identify where your audience spends the most time. For instance, if you're targeting professionals and B2B clients, LinkedIn might be your go-to platform. If your audience consists of millennials or Gen Z, platforms like Instagram or TikTok could be more suitable.

Analyze competitor presence:
Assessing your competitors' social media presence can provide valuable insights into platform effectiveness. Identify which platforms your competitors are active on and how they engage with their audience. If they're achieving significant traction on platforms like Facebook or X (Twitter), it could indicate that these platforms are worth investing in for your business as well.

Evaluate available resources:
Consider the resources at your disposal, including team expertise, budget and tools. Different platforms require varying levels of time and effort to manage effectively. If you lack resources for producing high-quality visual content,

platforms like TikTok may not be feasible in the short term. Assess your team's capabilities and determine which platforms align with your existing resources.

Define platform purpose:
Each social media platform should serve a distinct purpose tailored to your target audience and business goals. For example, if your goal is to showcase visual content to a younger demographic, platforms like Instagram or TikTok excel in visual storytelling. However, if your objective is to engage in professional networking or share industry insights, LinkedIn might be more suitable. Match your target audiences to different social media platforms, as appropriate.

Immerse yourself in social media:
To make informed decisions, immerse yourself in social media platforms to understand their functionalities and user dynamics. Just as you wouldn't advertise on a radio station without understanding its audience, don't approach social media blindly. Regularly engage with platforms relevant to your business to stay updated on trends and best practices.

Adapt and iterate:
Social media is dynamic, and your platform selection should reflect changing trends and business needs. Continuously evaluate your chosen platforms' performance against your goals and adjust your activities accordingly. Be open to adding new platforms or discontinuing underperforming ones based on evolving circumstances.

The importance of social media listening

Co-founder of Microsoft, Bill Gates, once remarked *'Your most unhappy customers are your greatest source of learning.'* These words encapsulate a profound truth in the world of business. While customer dissatisfaction may initially feel like a setback, it carries invaluable lessons that can propel a business towards improvement and growth. Unhappy customers provide a direct line to understanding pain points, identifying areas for enhancement, and refining products or services. Embracing their feedback not only demonstrates a commitment to customer-centricity but also fosters a culture of continuous improvement. In essence, these challenges become stepping stones for innovation, prompting businesses to evolve, adapt and ultimately deliver a superior customer experience.

To support this practice, social media listening emerges as an invaluable tool. Social media listening is the systematic process of tracking online conversations and extracting insights from user-generated content.

By monitoring platforms such as X, Facebook and LinkedIn, businesses can gain a comprehensive view of what their customers are discussing, sharing and feeling about their products, services or the industry at large.

Listening can be as simple as following your customers, following relevant hashtags, participating in online groups, or using sophisticated tools such as Brandwatch (www.brandwatch.com) or Pulsar (www.pulsarplatform.com) to unveil data regarding customer sentiments, emerging trends and even competitors' strategies.

It's useful to recognize that listening to your audience doesn't solely occur within the confines of the social media platforms you're actively using for communication. You can gather valuable insights by monitoring discussions and trends across various online channels, including social media platforms where you might not be actively posting content. For instance, a jeweller might utilize Pinterest to gauge the preferences of future brides when deciding which styles to promote in their Valentine's Day advertising campaign. By analyzing Pinterest boards and pins related to wedding planning and engagement ring styles, they could identify popular trends such as ring designs, gemstone choices and metal preferences. A software company developing a new productivity app might explore relevant subreddits on Reddit to understand user pain points, feature requests and competitor comparisons. By actively participating in discussions and observing feedback, they can gain valuable insights into user needs and preferences, informing their product development roadmap, marketing strategy and, at a tactical level, social media content.

Real-time awareness of conversations allows for agile decision-making, helping businesses to adapt their marketing activity in response to shifting consumer preferences or market dynamics, if required. Additionally, social media listening plays a pivotal role in brand perception management. Businesses can gauge how their brand is perceived by the public, identify key brand advocates and pinpoint areas that may require improvement. Through sentiment analysis, businesses can assess

Real-time awareness allows for agile decision-making

the impact of their marketing campaigns, product launches or public relations efforts.

Andy Lambert, founding team member and Director of Growth at ContentCal (sold to Adobe), acknowledges that social media listening is real 'in the weeds' social media activity but it was key to developing the business and scaling it from its foundation in 2016 through to its sale in 2021. He says, *'It's not glamorous, but it really works. I would encourage anyone looking to grow their business through social media marketing to embrace social media listening and take time to respond to messages that include both mentions of your own brand, but also competitor brands plus related industry and product keywords.'*

Chapter summary

At its core, impactful social media marketing starts with intimately knowing your customers. Their rational and emotional needs must anchor content, engagement and experiences. While reaching audiences at scale at speed has become infinitely easier in the digital world, cutting through the noise requires resonating deeply through relevance, value and meaning.

This chapter outlines foundational frameworks to guide strategy rooted in research, data and direct dialogue. Detailed customer personas bring quantitative insights to life while social listening provides qualitative feedback to continuously optimize efforts.

Choosing channels aligned to business goals and target audiences ensures contextual fit. Tailored and consistent content increases relevancy and memorability, securing that all-important mental real estate where growth begins.

There's no doubt that deepening your understanding of your customers unlocks a multitude of opportunities for business growth. It's time to start planning what that can look like...

Chapter 3

Planning your business growth

Business growth is not merely about making more money, nor is it solely about expanding your workforce or moving to bigger premises. Business growth is a strategic endeavour aimed at ensuring the long-term viability, relevance and competitiveness of your business. It's about ensuring that your business thrives and adapts in an ever-evolving market. Business growth contributes to a company's sustained success in various ways. It can result in increased market share, enhanced competitiveness, and more opportunities for innovation. Moreover, growth can provide financial stability and resilience, making your business less vulnerable to economic downturns and unforeseen challenges.

Growth *is* the goal of most businesses and is the reason behind many decisions that affect the daily workings of a company. Business growth is also intrinsically linked to personal growth, as your leadership and decision-making abilities evolve alongside your company. In 'Choosing to grow: The **Business growth is intrinsically linked to personal growth** leader's blueprint' McKinsey & Co suggests that driving sustainable, inclusive growth requires the right mindset, strategy and capabilities. They also suggest that growth is a 'choice'.

In this chapter, we will look at different types of business growth, different stages in a business's lifecycle, and strategies for pursuing business growth. We'll then examine the role marketing can play in business growth.

Organic and inorganic business growth

There are two basic forms of business growth: organic and inorganic. Organic growth involves expanding existing operations and increasing market share through internal development.

An exemplary case of a business that has experienced strong organic growth is Dyson, a technology company that specializes in designing and manufacturing a range of household appliances. Since the 1970s, Dyson has largely focused on research and technology development and growth through internal innovation and design.

By contrast, inorganic growth is driven by external activities, such as mergers and acquisitions. It involves integrating or merging with other businesses to achieve rapid expansion.

Mergers and acquisitions (M&A) offer several benefits to businesses, including accelerated growth, access to new markets and synergies that can drive operational efficiencies and cost savings. Additionally, M&A activities can provide opportunities for companies to acquire talent, intellectual property and technologies that complement their existing capabilities. They are common in the healthcare, financial services, retail and technology sectors. Facebook's acquisitions of Instagram and WhatsApp are prime examples of how a strategic M&A can bolster a company's competitive position and expand its product offerings and user base. However, navigating the M&A landscape comes with its challenges, including integration issues, cultural clashes between merging entities, regulatory hurdles and overvaluation risks. Effective due diligence, strategic planning, and post-merger integration efforts are essential to ensure the success of M&A transactions.

Although the mergers and acquisitions market dropped in 2023, largely due to high interest rates and economic uncertainty, the deal market was still valued at $3.2 trillion globally (Source: Bain & Company). It's a resilient sector and will continue to be significant in driving growth.

In practice, many businesses adopt a combination of both organic and inorganic growth strategies. They may first focus on maximizing organic growth potential before considering strategic acquisitions to complement their portfolio. Selecting the right growth strategy depends on factors such as the industry, market conditions, available resources and long-term business and personal objectives.

Setting growth objectives

In Chapter 1 we identified the importance of setting clear objectives for effective marketing, and the importance of those objectives being aligned with the business plan. The business plan is the driver for all activities within the business and should also include objectives and strategies for growth.

'Optimal growth is achieved only by a business being fully aligned, from ensuring that the sales, business development, and marketing strategies are not only in harmony with each other but are also driving towards the overarching business objectives. For instance, if

a business's primary objective is market expansion into a parallel segment, the marketing strategy should focus on brand awareness and lead generation within those identified new market segments. By ensuring that all commercial strategies are cohesively aligned with the business's growth objectives, organizations can create a more streamlined, effective approach to achieving their goals. I'd be so bold as to say that a good business strategy cannot be implemented without an aligned marketing strategy.'

Claire Hattrick, Fractional Marketing Director, TP03 Ltd

Common growth objectives include:

- **Revenue growth:** increasing annual revenue by a specific percentage or reaching a specific financial target.
- **Profit margin improvement:** enhancing your profit margin through cost optimization or pricing strategies.
- **New customer acquisition:** growing your customer base by a certain number or percentage increase.
- **Maximizing the value from existing customers:** increasing average order values (AOV) through cross-selling and upselling. Also increasing the long-term revenue from a customer by focusing on customer lifetime value (CTV), perhaps through exceptional customer service, nurturing customer loyalty to encourage additional purchases and reduce the opportunity for a customer to switch to a competitor.
- **Market leadership:** striving to become a market leader by surpassing competitors in terms of brand awareness and market share.

Don't forget to use the SMART acronym when setting objectives – it is essential that they always meet five criteria; that is that they are specific, measurable, achievable, relevant and time-related.

The importance of market share

Market share represents the portion of a specific market's total sales, revenue or customer base that a business (or its products/services) captures.

It is typically expressed as a percentage and is calculated by dividing a company's sales or revenue by the total sales or revenue of the entire market. For example, if a business's annual sales are $10 million, and the total sales of all businesses in its market amount to $100 million, that business's market share would be 10 per cent.

Market share serves as a useful gauge of a business's standing and competitiveness in its industry. A higher market share percentage signifies the popularity and success of a business (or its products or services) in the market. This metric goes beyond being a mere indicator; it offers valuable insights into a business's trajectory compared to its competitors, shedding light on opportunities for expansion or enhancements in marketing strategies. Beyond individual business (or product/service) analysis, keeping tabs on the overall market growth or decline is equally crucial. A decline in the overall market signals a call to action, urging businesses to diversify or explore new income streams to ensure resilience and sustained relevance. In essence, market share emerges as a compass guiding strategic decisions and highlighting the health of both individual companies and the industry at large.

It should be noted that growth is hard for businesses to achieve. In their study of the growth patterns and performance of the world's 5,000 largest public companies over the past 15 years, McKinsey & Company found that a typical company grew at 2.8 per cent per year during the ten years preceding Covid-19, and only one in eight recorded growth rates of more than 10 per cent per year. Their report on the findings, 'What matters most? Eight priorities for CEOs in 2024' suggests that *companies that manage to win market share away from competitors are likely to beat the growth expectations reflected in their share price, unlocking even stronger returns.*'

Understanding business development stages and their impact on growth

The choice of growth objectives is not static and should align with the business's current stage and market conditions. All

All businesses progress through stages of development

businesses progress through stages of development; introduction, growth, maturity and decline. This is illustrated in Figure 3.1 below. This developmental journey mirrors a natural lifecycle, where each stage introduces distinct challenges and opportunities. Recognizing and understanding these stages is crucial to determining which strategies to implement, and when. By doing so, businesses can maximize their chances of success and resilience in an ever-changing environment.

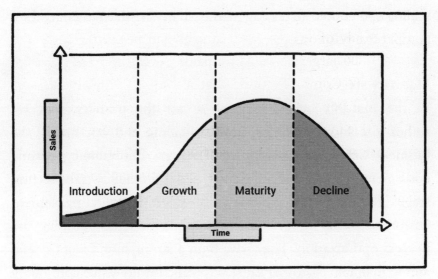

FIGURE 3.1 STAGES OF THE BUSINESS DEVELOPMENT LIFECYCLE

The different stages of business development are:

Introduction stage:
During the introduction phase, businesses are like seeds freshly planted in the soil. Their primary focus revolves around survival and establishing a foothold in the market. At this stage, the central objective is to gain initial customers, generate revenue and validate their value proposition.

From 2022–23, there were around 801,000 new UK businesses – an increase of 6.4 per cent from the previous year (Source: Money .co.uk).

Growth stage:
As businesses navigate the tumultuous introduction phase and find their stride, they transition into the growth stage. This stage is akin to the adolescence of a company when it experiences rapid expansion and development. Now, the focus shifts towards

scaling operations, increasing market share and strengthening their competitive position.

Maturity stage:

In the maturity stage, survival is not the primary concern; rather, the focus turns towards sustaining and optimizing the business. Customer acquisition still matters, but retaining existing customers, operational efficiency and profitability take centre stage. Businesses in the maturity stage typically implement customer loyalty programmes, cost-reduction programmes and process optimization. They have built a strong brand identity and aim to maintain customer satisfaction and loyalty while continuing to reap the benefits of market presence.

Decline stage:

The decline stage, akin to the autumn of a company's lifecycle, is marked by diminishing market relevance and, often, reduced profitability. Here, the objectives shift from growth and optimization to adaptation and preservation. In a B2C context, businesses on the decline might need to downsize, diversify into new markets or explore alternative revenue streams. In the B2B sector, the focus could be on strategic shifts to counter declining core business operations. It is a stage of reflection and adaptation, where businesses must re-evaluate their role in the market and make decisions about their future trajectory.

Case study: IBM

An example of reversing the decline stage in a business's development can be seen in the case of IBM (International

Business Machines) during the early 1990s. During this period, IBM faced significant challenges, including declining market share, financial losses and a rapidly changing technology landscape.

Under the leadership of CEO Lou Gerstner, who took the helm in 1993, IBM underwent a dramatic transformation. Gerstner shifted the company's focus from hardware to services and software, recognizing the emerging importance of consulting and IT services. IBM embraced a more customer-centric approach and initiated a cultural shift within the business to foster innovation and agility.

This strategic pivot, combined with divestitures of non-core businesses and a focus on emerging technologies, contributed to IBM's successful turnaround. By the late 1990s, IBM had not only stabilized its financial position but had also positioned itself as a leader in the growing IT services and consulting industry.

Today, IBM continues to adapt to the evolving tech landscape, embracing advancements such as cloud computing and Artificial Intelligence. Find out more at www.ibm.com

Recognizing when a business moves from one stage of development to another is not a straightforward process; the shift is typically gradual rather than a sudden transformation. It can also take steps back, as well as going forward through the development lifecycle. Nevertheless, there are various tell-tale signs and factors that business leaders can observe to understand this transition.

One critical indicator is the financial aspect. Changes in revenue and profitability often signify a shift between stages. For instance, as a business moves from the introduction phase to the growth stage, there's frequently a noticeable increase in revenue, reflecting an expanding customer base and market share. Conversely, a move towards the decline stage might be marked by reduced profits, which can be attributed to market saturation or changing customer preferences.

Market dynamics also play a pivotal role. An increase or decrease in market share can signal a transition. In the growth stage, for example, businesses typically witness heightened competition as they strive to capture more market share. In contrast, entry into the decline phase might entail losing market share due to a shrinking market or increased competition from newer players.

Moreover, the customer base evolves over time as the business moves through developmental stages. Businesses at the introduction phase tend to focus on customer acquisition, resulting in a dynamic and fluid clientele. In contrast, mature businesses often shift their emphasis towards customer retention and the cultivation of a loyal customer base, denoting a transition to a more stable growth phase.

The customer base evolves over time

Expanding the product or service portfolio can also denote movement between stages. Businesses at the introduction phase frequently commence with a limited range of offerings, while mature businesses often diversify their portfolios to cater to varied customer needs.

Various other factors come into play, including changes in operational complexity, shifts in market awareness and the nature of funding and investment. External influences, such as technological advancements or economic fluctuations, can further prompt transitions between stages.

What indicators do you have in place to identify the stages of your business development? Will you be ready to respond?

Case Study: Nintendo

In the early 2000s, Nintendo faced tough competition in the video game industry. Its GameCube console had underperformed, and its market share was dwindling. Sony's PlayStation and Microsoft's Xbox were dominating the gaming market.

Nintendo's revival and return to the growth stage can be attributed to several key strategies and innovations:

Wii console: In 2006, Nintendo launched the Wii, a groundbreaking gaming console with motion-sensing controllers. This innovation revolutionized the gaming industry, making gaming more accessible to a broader audience, including casual gamers and families. The Wii's success boosted Nintendo's market share and revenues.

Portable gaming: Nintendo's handheld gaming devices, such as the Nintendo DS and later the Nintendo 3DS, continued to perform well. These portable consoles captured a significant share of the handheld gaming market.

Iconic franchises: Nintendo capitalized on its iconic franchises, including Mario, Zelda and Pokémon, by releasing critically acclaimed games and merchandise. These franchises maintained a strong fanbase and attracted new players.

Digital distribution: Nintendo embraced digital distribution platforms, like the Nintendo eShop, to sell games and content directly to players.

Innovative game design: Nintendo's unique approach to game design and storytelling set it apart. Titles like 'Super Mario Galaxy' and 'The Legend of Zelda: Breath of the Wild' received critical acclaim and commercial success.

Global expansion: Nintendo continued to expand globally, targeting emerging markets like China and focusing on unique gaming experiences, such as theme parks.

Nintendo's remarkable turnaround demonstrates the significance of innovation, a deep understanding of customer preferences, and the ability to reinvent and revitalize established brands. By reimagining the gaming experience and expanding their reach, Nintendo transitioned from a period of decline to a robust return to the growth stage.

Strategies for growth

The Ansoff Matrix, named after its creator, Russian–American mathematician and business manager Igor Ansoff, is a strategic framework that provides a structured approach for businesses to contemplate and strategize their growth ambitions.

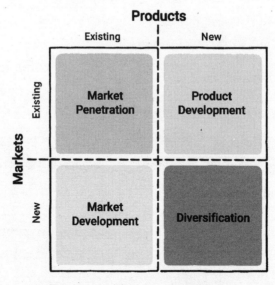

FIGURE 3.2 THE ANSOFF MATRIX

The Ansoff Matrix, pictured above, revolves around two fundamental dimensions: products/services (what a business offers) and markets (who the business serves). These dimensions create a matrix with four distinct growth strategies:

Market penetration: In this strategy, a business seeks to increase its market share by selling more of its existing products or services to its current customer base. This may involve tactics like price-related offers, or customer loyalty programmes. Market penetration is often the least risky of the four growth strategies because it leverages the businesses existing strengths.

Market development: This approach involves introducing existing products or services to new markets. It may entail entering different geographic regions, targeting new customer segments, or identifying untapped distribution channels. Market development seeks to expand the businesses customer base without altering its core offerings significantly.

Case study: Stitch Fix

Founded in 2011, Stitch Fix, renowned for its personalized styling service, started with women's fashion – and later successfully implemented a market development strategy for growth by introducing a men's fashion category, maternity wear and children's clothing. Customers fill out a styling profile online and a Stitch Fix stylist chooses items to send them. A styling fee gets credited towards anything purchased. Once received, the customer has three days to choose which items are worth keeping and which ones to return. The Stitch Fix business model is based on providing personalized styling and recommendation services to its customers through the use of stylists, supported by data scientists and machine learning algorithms to allow them to stay up-to-date with latest trends and support customer preferences. Stitch Fix offers a subscription service called the Annual Style Pass, which is available to the company's most loyal customers.

While the business continues to be successful, during the first quarter of fiscal year 2024 Stitch Fix ceased operations in the UK due to changes in the macroeconomic environment. In December 2023 CEO Matt Baer shared that Stitch Fix would 'continue to focus on optimizing the business in the short term while working to reimagine our business and operating model with the goal of delivering sustainable and profitable growth in the future'. This highlights the need to continually evaluate environmental factors when pursuing growth.

Product development: In this strategy, a business focuses on creating and launching new products or services aimed at its existing customer base. This typically involves innovation and research and development (R&D) efforts to meet changing customer needs or preferences. By doing so, the business aims to cross-sell to its current customers.

One example of a business that has pursued a product development strategy is The VA Handbook, discussed in detail in the success stories in Chapter 8. Owner Joanne Munro has a portfolio of products including e-courses and a membership. By increasing customer loyalty and nurturing a fanbase, Jo has been able to cross- and up-sell new products to existing customers. Similarly, Partner in Wine – another of the success stories covered in Chapter 8 – has extended their product line to include additional colour options as well as additional products.

Diversification: The diversification growth strategy is the most daring of the four. It involves introducing entirely new products or services to new markets. This strategy carries the highest risk but offers the potential for substantial rewards if successful. Diversification is often seen as a means of safeguarding against market fluctuations or seizing entirely new growth opportunities.

Case study: Amazon

Amazon is a leading example of diversification. What began as an online bookseller in 1994, Amazon has diversified its product and service portfolio to an astonishing extent. Amazon now offers cloud computing services through Amazon Web Services (AWS), operates physical stores like Whole Foods, produces its content through Amazon Studios, and manufactures hardware like Kindle e-readers and Echo smart speakers.

In its pursuit for diversification, Amazon developed key partnerships and acquired many other businesses. This includes acquiring the online music retailer CD Now to give its users a wider selection of music titles, clothing retailer Shopbop to expand its clothing line, and video gaming company Twitch Interactive to improve its gaming products.

Amazon's aim is to be 'Earth's most customer-centric company'. Its mission is to continually raise the bar of the customer experience by using the Internet and technology to help customers find, discover and buy anything, and empower businesses and content creators to maximize their success. In 2023, net sales reached $574.8 billion. Amazon delivers to Prime members at the fastest speeds ever globally, with more than 7 billion orders in 2023 arriving the same or next day.

Potential barriers to business growth

Several potential barriers can impede business growth, ranging from internal challenges to external factors. Internally, insufficient resources, operational inefficiencies or a lack of scalable processes may hinder a business's ability to expand. External factors such as economic downturns, regulatory changes or intense market competition can also pose substantial challenges.

As we saw with the example of Blockbuster in the previous chapter, businesses that fail to grow ultimately stagnate and fail. In the case of Blockbuster, the business

Businesses that fail to grow ultimately stagnate

failed to address changes in the market and the shift from DVD to streaming. It didn't diversify its products or offerings, and ultimately its business model became obsolete.

Another example is Kodak, a renowned photography company. Kodak struggled to embrace the digital revolution in photography, despite inventing the first digital camera in 1975. The company's reluctance to transition from film to digital, fearing that it would cannibalize its existing film business, ultimately led to its decline.

Failure is an integral part of the business growth process and can offer valuable insights for businesses striving to expand. It is essential to have measures in place when pursuing business growth to identify signs of inefficacy early on. Implementing key performance indicators (KPIs), regularly assessing market responses and closely monitoring financial metrics can serve as effective measures. Recognizing when things aren't working and having the flexibility to pivot or make the decision to stop a particular initiative is crucial.

As we saw earlier with the Nintendo and IBM case studies, it is possible to turn things around when facing possible failure.

This strategic pivot, combined with divestitures of non-core businesses and a focus on emerging technologies, contributed to IBM's successful turnaround. By the late 1990s, IBM had not only stabilized its financial position but had also positioned itself as a leader in the growing IT services and consulting industry.

The role of marketing in business growth

Ask any trained marketer and they will quickly answer that their role is about much more than 'promotion', as it is so often perceived to be. A trained marketer will quickly respond with an explanation of how marketing encompasses a holistic approach to understanding, influencing and satisfying customer needs. Beyond promotion, it involves comprehensive research, strategic planning and the orchestration of various elements encapsulated by the foundational concept of the 4Ps: product, price, place and promotion.

In detailing the 4Ps, a marketer will emphasize that marketing begins with the intricacies of the product or service itself. This entails not only understanding its features but also aligning it with customer needs and desires. Pricing strategies come next, involving considerations of value perception, competitive positioning and overall market economics.

The 'place' component refers to the distribution channels and accessibility of the product, highlighting the importance of reaching the right audience at the right time and place. Lastly, while 'promotion' is a key element, a marketer will underscore that it goes beyond advertising (another perception). It involves crafting a compelling narrative, building brand identity and fostering emotional connections with the target audience.

Social media and the 4Ps

Social media complements and amplifies various aspects of the 4Ps. Social media plays a significant role in the 'promotion' aspect of the 4Ps, serving as a powerful channel for creating awareness, communicating messages and engaging with the target audience.

Social media also has implications for the 'product' aspect of the marketing mix. It serves as a platform for gathering insights into customer preferences, expectations and feedback. Businesses can leverage social media to conduct market research, solicit opinions and gain a deeper understanding of what features or improvements consumers desire in a product. Moreover, social media provides a direct channel ('place') for customer communication, allowing businesses to address concerns, answer queries and showcase the unique features or benefits of their products. In this way, social media contributes to shaping and refining the product offering based on real-time interactions and feedback from the target audience.

Social media influences pricing strategies through real-time feedback and market insights, and distribution channels (place) by facilitating online transactions and e-commerce.

Marketing simultaneously has a role to play in leading the external face of the business and, internally, the voice of the customer and other key stakeholders. This dual role means that marketing spans all stages of the business growth journey, from creating awareness through to encouraging customers to make a purchase and recommend your business to their peers, friends and family.

As businesses grow, marketing guides market research to identify new opportunities and minimize risks identified through a PESTLE or SWOT analysis (see Appendix 1 and 2). As the internal voice of the customer, marketing supports feedback and product development, ensuring products and services align with market demands.

As highlighted in Salesforce's State of Marketing research (2022), post-Covid-19, unlocking new customer segments and expanding geographical targets has become a key avenue for success. For marketers, this translates into both a challenge and an exciting opportunity. Embracing change and harnessing innovative tools and technologies, such as AI, are not just priorities but the driving forces behind a future where customer communications are expected to be digital-first and highly personalized.

Resources for growth

For businesses to harness the full potential of social media, they must allocate the necessary resources – people, tools and budget. Social media might be seen as easy and free to access, but to maximize the opportunities when using the platforms for business purposes, there are some resource requirements.

People: The social media team

A well-structured and capable social media team is the backbone of any successful social media marketing effort. The team's composition and roles can vary depending on the size and objectives of the business, but here are some key positions typically found in a social media team:

Social Media Manager: This individual oversees the entire social media portfolio of activity, including goal setting, content planning and performance analysis. They are responsible for ensuring that the social media efforts align with the overall marketing and business objectives.

Content Creators: Content is king in social media marketing. Content creators, which can include writers, designers, photographers and videographers, are responsible for crafting engaging and visually appealing content that resonates with the target audience.

Community Managers: Community managers are the frontline of engagement with the audience. They respond to comments, messages and interactions on social media platforms, fostering relationships with customers and addressing their concerns.

Data Analysts: Social media activity generates a wealth of data. Data analysts are responsible for monitoring key performance metrics, conducting competitive analysis and using data-driven insights to optimize social media campaigns.

Advertising Specialists: For paid social media campaigns, advertising specialists are crucial. They design, execute and manage paid ad campaigns across various platforms, ensuring they reach the right audience and meet performance goals.

Hootsuite's 2023 Social Media Career Report highlights the vast array of social media manager remits with only 11 per cent of social media managers having a role that primarily focuses on social; their roles are often split across other requirements. The range of roles outlined above might feel like an ambitious luxury for those marketers who are currently multi-tasking; however it's important to understand what the role requires and to understand how this is likely to change as your business grows. In the near future we are likely to see roles focused on individual platforms or niche social skills.

Tools: The Tech Arsenal

A wide array of tools and software can greatly enhance the efficiency and effectiveness of social media marketing efforts. These tools can streamline various aspects of social media management, from content creation to analytics and reporting.

Here are some essential categories of tools:

Content management and scheduling tools: Platforms like Hootsuite, Buffer and Sprout Social allow social media teams to plan, schedule and publish content across multiple social media channels from a single dashboard. These tools also provide analytics to track performance.

Content creation tools: Tools like Canva, Adobe and Animoto assist in creating visually compelling content, such as graphics, images and videos, that are optimized for social media.

Social media analytics tools: Tools like Semrush Social Tracker and Google Analytics provide in-depth insights into social media performance. They help track metrics like engagement rates, click-through rates and conversion rates, allowing teams to assess the effectiveness of their activities.

Social listening tools: Social listening tools like Brandwatch and Pulsar monitor social media channels for brand mentions, keywords and industry trends. They provide valuable insights into customer sentiment and emerging topics.

Paid social advertising platforms: For businesses running paid social campaigns, self-serve platforms like Meta Ads

Manager and LinkedIn Campaign Manager are indispensable. These platforms enable precise audience targeting and budget management.

Budget: Funding your social media efforts

Budget allocation is a critical aspect of social media marketing. It encompasses both organic (non-paid) and paid social media activities. The budget for social media marketing should be viewed as an investment, as it directly influences the reach, impact and return on investment (ROI) of your campaigns.

Here are key elements to consider:

Content creation and management: Allocating a portion of the budget for content creation and management ensures that you have high-quality, engaging content to share with your audience. This can include expenses for graphic design, video production and scheduling tools.

Advertising spend: If your strategy includes paid social media advertising, you'll need to allocate a budget for ad campaigns. The amount can vary widely depending on your objectives, audience size and the platforms you choose.

Community management: Monitoring and engaging with your audience on social media platforms requires human resources. These personnel costs should be considered in the budget, including the salaries of community managers and customer support staff.

Training and development: Staying up-to-date with the rapidly evolving social media landscape is essential. Allocating a budget for training and development ensures that your team can leverage the latest tools and tactics effectively.

Testing and experimentation: It's important to set aside a portion of the budget for testing and experimentation. This allows you to try out new approaches, analyze their performance, and refine your activities based on the results.

Performance analytics: Investing in analytics tools and resources to track the performance of your social media campaigns is crucial. This enables you to measure ROI and make data-driven decisions for optimization.

Crisis management: A portion of the budget should be reserved for unforeseen events or crises that may require immediate attention and response on social media.

Scaling: As your social media marketing efforts grow, you may need to allocate additional budget resources to accommodate increased content production, advertising spend and personnel.

Chapter summary

The process of planning business growth entails strategic thinking and a clear understanding of the stages of development. Key learnings from this process include recognizing that business growth involves more than just increasing revenue; it's about ensuring long-term viability, competitiveness and relevance. It's also crucial to understand the different types of growth – organic and inorganic – and the various strategies available, such as market penetration, market development, product development and diversification.

Marketing plays a vital role in driving business growth, encompassing more than just promotion. The 4Ps framework – product, price, place and promotion – guides marketing activities, with social media playing a crucial role in amplifying these efforts.

To leverage social media effectively, businesses need to allocate the necessary resources – people, tools and budget. A well-structured social media team, equipped with the right tools and adequate budget allocation, is essential for successful social media marketing efforts.

Chapter 4

The importance of branding

Imagine you're wandering through the streets of a new city, looking for a cup of coffee. You see a small local coffee shop and then you spot a Starbucks sign. Though both establishments may offer equally good coffee, you find yourself heading towards the iconic green logo. You might even pay more for the coffee in Starbucks versus the local coffee shop. Why? Because of the power of branding.

The American Marketing Association defines brand as *'a name, term, design, symbol, or any other feature that identifies one seller's goods or service as distinct from those of other sellers'*.

A brand guides you towards the immediate recognition of the swoosh on a pair of trainers or the golden arches of a fast-food giant that in turn triggers **A brand is more** associations with quality, reliability and a certain **than a logo** lifestyle.

It is important to recognize that a brand is more than a logo. It's more than a colour palette. Brand identity is both a visual and verbal expression, that aims to build an emotional connection.

Brands in the automotive market

In the automotive market, brands play a pivotal role in shaping customer perceptions and preferences. Customers often form strong emotional connections with automotive brands, making purchase decisions not only based on technical specifications, and price, but also on the brand's reputation and the lifestyle it represents.

What comes to mind when you consider the Porsche brand? How about Ford?

Porsche, the renowned German luxury sports car manufacturer, embodies a brand identity characterized by a rich heritage, unwavering commitment to performance and innovation, and a distinctive design language. The company's iconic models, such as the 911, reflect a balance of continuity and evolution, contributing to a timeless aesthetic. Porsche's positioning as a luxury brand is underscored by exclusivity, sophisticated marketing and a focus on high-end craftsmanship. The brand's success in motorsports, particularly at events like the 24 Hours of Le Mans, enhances its image of excellence. Beyond vehicles, Porsche cultivates a community and lifestyle, creating a holistic experience for enthusiasts. Overall, Porsche's brand identity is a harmonious fusion of tradition, innovation and a commitment to delivering a high-performance driving experience.

Ford embrace a brand identity centred on accessibility, reliability and innovation. With a legacy deeply rooted in the history of the American automotive industry, Ford emphasizes practicality in its vehicle design. While not pursuing luxury, Ford's commitment to innovation, demonstrated through advancements like electric and hybrid vehicles, highlights its ability to adapt to evolving consumer needs. The brand's enduring presence is tied to its role as a provider of dependable vehicles for a broad demographic, making it a recognizable and trusted name in the automotive landscape.

A car satisfies a fundamental need for transportation, and perhaps convenience over public transport.

However, each automotive brand carries a distinct identity, embodying a unique combination of design, performance and values. Whether renowned for innovation, luxury, reliability or a blend of these attributes, automotive brands evoke a sense of lifestyle and aspiration.

Like me, perhaps your first car was a Ford, and right now you are experiencing the feeling of nostalgia. Perhaps you aspire to own a Porsche one day and have started daydreaming about driving hairpin bends in Italy.

Clearly, automotive branding is about far more than their logos.

The concept of brand can also be applied to individuals. There may or may not be visual associations in terms of logos and colours, but there are feelings associated with personal brands. Whether that's a highly recognized individual such as Diary of a CEO podcast host Stephen Bartlett, founder of *The Huffington Post*, Arianna Huffington, or someone who is a leading voice in your industry sector.

As part of your business growth plans you should consider the role of both your business brand, the branding of your products and services, and the personal brands of your team. As we will discover shortly, these are valuable assets and key drivers of growth.

Differentiation and value propositions

Where competition in a marketplace can be fierce, branding serves as a tool for differentiation.

Differentiation, within the realm of marketing strategy, represents a nuanced and strategic approach aimed at establishing a product or brand as distinctive amidst your sea of competitors, often allowing a business to command a premium price and build customer loyalty.

The concept of differentiation finds its roots in prominent academic models and theories, with Michael Porter's Generic Strategies standing out as a foundational framework that explores the role of differentiation in achieving and sustaining competitive advantage. Porter outlines that strategy targets either cost leadership, differentiation or focus. A business must only choose one of the three areas or risk getting 'stuck in the middle'. Find out more about this framework in Appendix 4.

The concept of value propositions intersects with Michael Porter's Generic Strategies framework and the concept of differentiation. In his book, *Malcolm McDonald on Value Propositions*, McDonald and his co-author emphasize the importance of understanding and effectively communicating the value that a product or service provides to its customers.

A value proposition is the unique combination of benefits that a business offers to address the needs and desires of its target market. It answers the question: 'Why should customers choose our product or service over competitors' offerings?' McDonald and Grant Oliver highlight that a compelling value proposition is essential for attracting customers and achieving sustainable competitive advantage. It involves identifying customers' key pain points and desires, articulating how the product or service addresses these needs better than alternatives, and clearly communicating this value to the target audience.

For example, Nike's value proposition is 'to provide fashionable, innovative and high-performance shoes for customers in every sport to meet their changing demands'. Coca-Cola's value proposition is 'to provide refreshment and enjoyment to people of all ages and demographics worldwide'.

Can you define your value proposition? McDonald's book will help you do this.

The brand promise

I often reflect on the definition of brand used within my first agency employer: 'a brand is a promise consistently delivered'.

The 'promise' being the way in which a value proposition is communicated externally to customers.

Answer these questions quickly. What colour do you associate with the drink Coca-Cola? Can you recall the brand taglines for L'Oréal haircare products or a KitKat chocolate bar?[1]

No doubt you have seen these products multiple times. We can also make associations with experiences. Let's return to one of my favourites – coffee drinking.

Starbucks have successfully turned a simple cup of coffee into a brand experience. The comfortable seating, mellow lighting and even the carefully curated music playlist create an inviting atmosphere that lures you in. No matter which store you visit, you can expect the same quality, the same taste and the same experience. This experience breeds trust. Customers

---

[1] Coca-Cola is synonymous with the colour red. L'Oréal's tagline is 'Because you're worth it.' KitKat's tagline is 'Have a break, have a KitKat.'

are willing to pay more for a Starbucks coffee because they know exactly what they're getting – a reliable and satisfying coffee experience.

These associations and quick recall do not happen overnight. Branding is not a one-off exercise. It's an ongoing process that requires consistent application and repetition. It involves all touchpoints a customer has with a business, and therefore is not the sole responsibility of the marketing department. When a brand consistently delivers on its promise customers are re-assured of their decisions.

Branding is not a one-off exercise

Brand strength

The Brand Resonance Pyramid, or Customer-Based Brand Equity (CBBE) model, developed by Kevin Lane Keller in his textbook *Strategic Brand Management*, outlines the process through which customers build and evaluate brand equity. It is illustrated with permission from the author in Figure 4.1 below.

Brand equity refers to the intangible value and strength that a brand adds to a product or service. It is the result of a combination of factors such as brand awareness, brand loyalty, perceived quality and associations customers have with the brand. A brand with high equity has a positive reputation, is trusted by customers, and often commands higher prices than similar products without a strong brand. Brand equity is a strategic asset for businesses, representing the overall health and competitive advantage derived from customer perceptions and experiences associated with the brand.

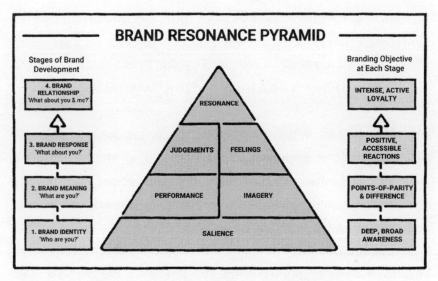

FIGURE 4.1 THE BRAND RESONANCE PYRAMID

The model identifies four key stages of brand development, representing four fundamental questions that your customers will ask – often subconsciously – about your brand.

Brand identity: Who are you? This is the fundamental stage where we, as marketers, need to establish a clear and distinctive brand identity by creating awareness and defining salience (how easily and often the brand comes to mind).

Brand meaning: What are you? At this stage, customers are seeking to create meaningful associations. This step involves brand performance and brand imagery. The objective is to identify points of parity and difference.

- Performance defines how well your product meets your customers' needs. According to Keller's model, performance consists of five categories: primary characteristics and features; product reliability, durability and serviceability;

service effectiveness, efficiency and empathy; style and design; and price.

- Imagery refers to how well your brand meets your customers' needs on a social and psychological level.

Brand response: What about you? Marketers seek to cultivate positive customer responses to the brand. This involves creating the right judgements (consumer opinions about the brand), attitudes (consumer feelings and preferences towards the brand), and perceptions of brand quality and credibility.

Brand relationship: What about you and me? The final stage aims for a deep, emotional connection between the brand and its customers. At this level, the brand achieves resonance by creating an intense, active loyalty where customers not only prefer the brand but also feel a sense of community and engagement with it.

Keller breaks this relationship down into four categories:

- Behavioural loyalty – this includes regular, repeat purchases.
- Attitudinal attachment – your customers love your brand or your product, and they see it as a special purchase.
- Sense of community – your customers feel a sense of community with people associated with the brand, including other customers and business representatives.
- Active engagement – this is the strongest example of brand loyalty. Customers are actively engaged with your brand, even when they are not purchasing it or consuming it. This could include joining a group related to the brand, participating in online events, or taking part in other brand-related activities.

Case study: Learning from rebranding fails

Rebranding is a strategic move that companies undertake to rejuvenate their image, connect with evolving consumer preferences, or signal a transformation. However, not all rebranding efforts yield the desired outcomes. In fact, some can backfire, leading to negative publicity, loss of consumer trust and financial setbacks.

Two notable examples of rebranding failures are Royal Mail and Gap.

Royal Mail, the UK's universal postal service provider, embarked on a rebranding journey in 2001. The business sought to modernize its image and demonstrate its commitment to innovation. However, the decision to rename the business 'Consignia' was met with widespread criticism and confusion. Recognizing the misstep, less than a year later Royal Mail reverted to its original name.

Similarly, retailer Gap faced a backlash following its attempted rebranding in 2010. The business, known for its classic apparel and iconic logo, unveiled a new logo design as part of a broader brand overhaul. However, the minimalist design deviated significantly from Gap's traditional aesthetic, alienating loyal customers and sparking outcry on social media platforms. Within days, Gap reversed its decision, reinstating the original logo and acknowledging the importance of preserving brand heritage and engaging stakeholders in the rebranding process.

Employer branding

Employer branding refers to the process of shaping and promoting a business's reputation as an employer of choice. It encompasses the company's values, culture and employee experiences, as well as its efforts to attract, engage and retain top talent. A strong employer brand not only attracts qualified candidates to join the business but also fosters employee loyalty and advocacy, ultimately contributing to business success and growth.

Employee advocacy, the practice of empowering employees to promote the company's brand and offerings on their personal social media channels, is a powerful tool for bolstering employer branding efforts.

Statistics from the LinkedIn Official Guide to Employee Advocacy underscore the value of this approach. On average, employees have ten times more 1st-degree connections on LinkedIn than a

Employee advocacy is a powerful tool

company page has followers, making them powerful amplifiers of the company's message. Additionally, content shared by employees is eight times more likely to engage audiences and 24 times more likely to be reshared compared to content shared by brands. Content shared by employees is clicked through twice as often, indicating higher effectiveness in driving website traffic and engagement.

Implementing an employee advocacy programme involves providing training and ongoing support to ensure that employees effectively represent the business online. This can include offering preapproved content for sharing, such as blog posts or infographics, and recognizing and rewarding employees who actively participate in advocacy efforts.

Case study: Marriott International

Marriott International has 8,100+ hotel properties and 31 top hotel brands across 138 countries and territories. And they are still growing.

The employment brand team at Marriott International started their new employer brand initiative by conducting interviews with associates in every region, brand, job family and demographic. With 200+ pages of findings, they identified 13 major themes, and eventually this turned into three brand pillars – begin, belong and become.

The 'Be' brand, launched in April 2023, has the goal of attracting and retaining top talent, to empower associates to fulfil their career goals, further Marriott's commitment to creating a culture of inclusion, and offer innovative opportunities to grow professionally and personally.

In their announcement for the new brand, Anthony Capuano, President and Chief Executive Officer of Marriott International said, 'As we focus on strengthening our culture, expanding our global workforce, and positioning the company for continued growth, we are excited to build on our people-first culture with Be. We are proud to be an employer of choice for hundreds of thousands of associates who wear the Marriott name badge around the world. Be will help us fulfil our purpose of connecting people through the power of travel by empowering and supporting our associates.'

Social media and brand communications

There's no doubt that social media can have a profound influence on brand image and reputation. Positive comments, reviews and posts can significantly boost a brand's reputation, while negative feedback and criticism can damage it. As we discovered in Chapter 2, social media has a key role to play in terms of customer care and this is often the first engagement touchpoint with a brand.

A social media presence allows businesses to showcase their credibility and trustworthiness, and for customers to share experiences, opinions and perceptions.

Reputation is everything

Reputation is everything, especially when economic environments are challenging. As we learned earlier, trust is a core ingredient of every buying decision and trust is dependent on reputation.

Setting up social media profiles requires assets to support the brand – from header images, to descriptions in the about/bio sections. For up-to-date social media profile set-up checklists, visit www.luanwise .co.uk/books/smartsocialmedia or scan the QR code below.

Establishing brand guidelines within your business is useful for maintaining consistency and professionalism across all online interactions. These guidelines should include information relating to both visual and written content. Every social media post needs to connect back to the messages the brand wants to convey to its target audience. Every social media interaction, whether it is a detailed reply to a complaint or a thank-you message following a favourable review, can serve to reinforce a positive brand image. This applies to all content associated with your business – whether it's from a centrally co-ordinated corporate account or an employee profile.

Case study: Aldi – the most famous supermarket on social media

When Covid-19 first hit in 2020, the supermarket chain Aldi began to lose market share versus its big four rivals. In response they decided to switch their use of social media from a tactical performance channel towards a brand-building goal of making Aldi the most famous supermarket on social media.

Working with McCann Manchester, Aldi's combined impressions grew from 2.6 million in 2019 to more than 764 million by 2022. Their social media activity is known for funny, relatable content which often includes trending events and an unforgettable online battle with other retailers over an alleged intellectual property dispute about a caterpillar cake.

In September 2022, Aldi regained market share to overtake Morrisons as the UK's fourth-largest supermarket. They were also awarded winner of the 2023 Marketing Week Award for Long Term Brand Building Excellence, the first time a brand has ever won the prize for social activity. The accolade was based on a public vote plus the views of a judging panel of senior marketing leaders.

Follow Aldi on Facebook, Instagram, X (Twitter) and TikTok @AldiUK

Brand building is a critical aspect of establishing a strong and enduring presence in a market, fostering customer loyalty and shaping positive perceptions. However, the effectiveness of brand-building activities may take time to translate into tangible sales. To bridge this gap and drive more immediate results, sales activation becomes essential. Sales activation involves tactical and short-term marketing activities aimed at stimulating immediate customer action, such as making a purchase.

It focuses on leveraging promotions, discounts and other persuasive techniques to encourage consumers to act promptly. The concept of the *Long and the Short of It*, as proposed in the book of the same name by marketing effectiveness experts Peter Field and Les Binet, underscores the importance of balancing both brand building and sales activation activities. Their research emphasizes that an optimal marketing strategy involves a harmonious blend of long-term brand building for sustained growth and short-term sales activation for immediate impact, creating a well-rounded approach that maximizes overall marketing effectiveness.

'The Long and the Short of It'

The study by Les Binet and Peter Field reviewed the Institute of Practitioners in Advertising (IPA) Databank of 996 campaigns entered into the IPA Effectiveness Awards between 1980 and 2010. In 2019 LinkedIn commissioned Binet and Field to study the same issues in a B2B context.

The research establishes a 60/40 rule of thumb – this is the idea that you should be spending around 60 per cent of your budget on brand building, and the remaining 40 per cent on sales activation. This is not a hard and fast rule, however – with different circumstances the balance could be different.

For example, for financial services they **Branding takes time** recommend 80 per cent brand building; for B2B an almost perfect 50:50 split; for not-for-profit 44 per cent brand, 56 per cent activation.

However, Binet and Field argue that brand awareness isn't enough; it's important that people know about you, but it's even more important to build on this and create levels of brand salience (the degree to which your brand is thought of or noticed). But branding takes time, and businesses often have immediate targets to meet. This is why marketers need to balance the long-term, big picture activity, with short, targeted campaigns designed to generate demand and sales. Figure 4.2 below illustrates the importance of brand building for long-term sales growth alongside sales activation activity for short-term sales uplifts.

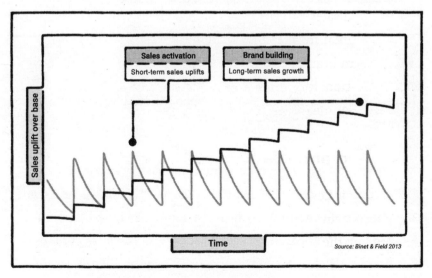

FIGURE 4.2 'THE LONG AND THE SHORT OF IT'

According to marketing expert Mark Ritson, who advocates the research as part of his Mini MBA marketing and brand management courses, 'The most important word in *The Long and the Short of It* is *"and"*.'

Using social media to 'hum, sing and shout'

Another way to view the 'long and the short of it', and as a useful structure for planning social media content, is the hum-sing-shout framework used by LinkedIn and illustrated in Figure 4.3 below.

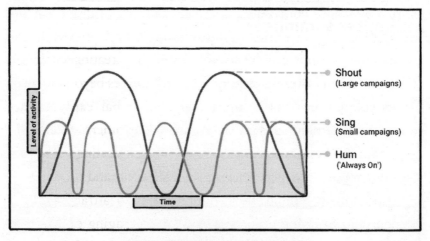

FIGURE 4.3 HUM, SING, SHOUT

Hum-sing-shout is the overlap of usually three levels of marketing activity:

- **Hum** is for 'always-on' content designed to run continuously throughout the year. Hum content is valuable and can provide a 'warm-up' context for campaign-based content.
- **Sing** is for campaign-based content, this occurs less frequently throughout the year. It may be related to sales activation campaigns.

- **Shout** is big, broad content, it occurs less frequently than 'sing' content and may be used for product launches or key events.

This framework ensures a balanced approach to social media content, maintaining consistent engagement (hum), driving focused campaign initiatives (sing), and generating impactful moments (shout) to amplify brand messaging and achieve marketing objectives.

Chapter summary

Branding is a powerful tool for businesses, creating distinct identities and fostering customer loyalty. It goes beyond logos and colours, encompassing visual and verbal expressions that build emotional connections with customers. Effective branding involves differentiation, communicating unique value propositions, and delivering consistent brand promises.

Additionally, employer branding is key to attracting top talent and fostering employee loyalty. Leveraging employee advocacy through social media amplifies employer branding efforts, turning employees into important brand ambassadors.

Effective branding and strategic use of social media, as part of a balanced approach to marketing activities, are essential for businesses to cultivate strong brand equity, foster customer loyalty and drive sustainable growth.

Chapter 5

Guiding the buyer's journey with social media content

In this chapter, we will examine the role social media marketing has to play during the buyer's journey; in particular, how social media uses storytelling and engagement to guide a potential buyer through their decision-making process.

The buyer's journey refers to the path that a potential customer takes to make their decision, from initial awareness of a problem or need to the ultimate purchase of a solution or product.

Throughout the journey a business can influence a potential customer

Throughout the journey a business can influence a potential customer by providing valuable, timely and relevant content. Content can take various forms, including text, images, videos, infographics and other multimedia interactive elements.

So, why is social media so instrumental in the buying journey?

28.7 per cent of Internet users aged 16 to 64 discover new brands, products and services via advertisements on social media; 23 per cent cite comments on social media as a source of brand discovery. Finding content online (e.g. articles, videos) is the primary purpose for 30.2 per cent of social media users, along with finding inspiration for things to do and buy (26.7

per cent) and work-related networking or research (21.3 per cent). This tendency to use social media for discovery is higher among younger age groups, where use of social networks is now overtaking search engines such as Google and Bing as a source of information when researching brands. (Source: DataReportal, January 2024). The role of social media is now extending far beyond keeping in touch with friends and family, and in providing entertainment.

Social media and stages in the buyer's journey

As we saw in Chapter 1, Figure 1.1, the buying decision process begins with potential customers becoming aware of a business and its offering. As they move to generate a deeper level of interest and desire, a potential customer is at the stage of consideration. Finally, the journey concludes with a taking of action, most likely a purchase.

In the awareness stage, potential customers become aware of a challenge or need they have. This is the earliest point in the journey, where they might be experiencing symptoms of a problem but haven't yet identified a solution. To guide them, businesses can use social media to create content that addresses common pain points and introduces their brand as a potential solution. For example, a fitness equipment company targeting individuals seeking healthier lifestyles might share informative blog posts about the benefits of regular exercise or post engaging workout videos demonstrating proper workout techniques. These content pieces, when shared on platforms like Facebook, Instagram and TikTok, not only capture the attention of the target audience but also position the brand as a knowledgeable and supportive resource in the early stages of their journey. If a potential customer is not yet aware of a problem, your content could stimulate a need for your products or services!

Moving into the consideration stage, potential buyers have now defined their problem and are actively seeking solutions. This is where businesses can further nurture these prospects through social media content that explores the benefits and features of their products or services. Providing in-depth guides or comparison charts – such as infographics highlighting the importance of a balanced fitness routine – can be instrumental in helping potential customers evaluate their options.

Case study: HubSpot

HubSpot, a well-known inbound marketing and sales software business, excels in guiding potential B2B buyers through the consideration stage with an ecosystem of educational content and community support. HubSpot has 194,000+ customers in 120+ countries and a community of more than 150 user groups in 21 countries.

On social media, they post links to blog articles, whitepapers and webinars related to inbound marketing, content strategy, SEO and more.

These resources offer valuable insights and best practices in the digital marketing world, while helping potential customers understand the features and benefits of HubSpot's software, positioning it as a strong contender in their decision-making process.

When potential customers are ready to make a purchase, social media content can play a pivotal role in the final push by offering testimonials, product demonstrations and limited-time offers. Through platforms like Instagram and Pinterest, visually appealing content can showcase products in real-world situations, helping prospects envision themselves as satisfied customers.

Guiding the buyer's journey with social media content is about recognizing the stages of the decision-making process and aligning your messaging accordingly. By creating content that resonates with potential customers at each phase, businesses can leverage social media to influence purchasing decisions, establish trust and build enduring relationships with their audience.

Businesses can leverage social media to influence purchasing decisions

The Content Marketing Matrix by Smart Insights (www .smartinsights.com), illustrated below in Figure 5.1, is a useful mapping tool for planning which types of content will support the path to purchase.

The two dimensions in this matrix are:

1. Awareness through to purchase, shown on the horizontal axis.
2. Emotional to rational content engagement formats available, shown on the vertical axis.

As you read from left to right the matrix shows how different content assets can develop audience awareness and reach through to purchase. More visual, interactive content to support emotional buying triggers is shown at the top of the matrix with more static content at the bottom supporting rational decision-making.

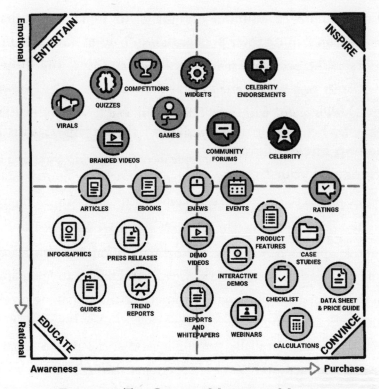

FIGURE 5.1 THE CONTENT MARKETING MATRIX

Mastering the art of storytelling across the buyer's journey

The buyer's journey is not a linear path from awareness to consideration and decision; it's a dynamic narrative where potential customers engage with your brand and might need to encounter it several times before they decide to buy. Storytelling, a potent tool that amplifies the impact of your social media content at each stage of the buyer's journey, involves crafting compelling narratives that resonate with your audience. It goes beyond presenting facts and features; it encapsulates the essence of your brand, creating that important emotional connection with your audience.

Lucy Hitchcock, founder of Partner in Wine – the success story featured in Chapter 8 – confirms: *'If your brand has a good story behind it, people are more likely to get on board. That's exactly why Partner in Wine experienced the growth it had in its first year: people got on board with how I started it due to a problem I faced during the pandemic that many other people were facing while pubs and bars were closed!'*

Storytelling encapsulates the essence of your brand

Through storytelling, brands can convey their values, mission and the real-world impact of their products or services. This narrative approach not only captures attention but also leaves a lasting impression, fostering a sense of authenticity and relatability that can influence a potential customer's decision-making process. Whether it's sharing success stories, behind-the-scenes glimpses, or customer testimonials, storytelling on social media creates a cohesive and memorable brand experience throughout the buyer's journey.

In the awareness stage, storytelling becomes a compelling way to introduce your brand as the hero who understands the challenges your audience faces. Potential customers often face problems they're struggling to define. To guide them, businesses can create stories that illustrate common challenges and their consequences. By sharing relatable narratives, your content can demonstrate empathy and expertise. For example, if you're selling project management software, share a story about a team that missed a crucial deadline because of disorganization, showcasing the impact it had on the project.

As people spend time getting to know your brand, they will transition into the consideration stage. Then it's time to delve deeper into the narrative, sharing stories of how your products or services provide solutions, the benefits they bring, and the tangible impact they've had on previous customers. Your storytelling should be designed to guide prospects in their evaluation process, making it easier for them to recognize your brand as the trusted guide in their journey.

An authentic and compelling business story can be a game-changer, connecting with your audience on a deeper level and setting you apart from the competition. But where do you start?

Every business has a beginning – a founding journey with struggles, 'a-ha' moments and human elements that make your brand relatable. Sharing this story can be a powerful tool in your social media arsenal. Turn to the success stories in Chapter 8 to see how a strong founder story helped to build Evoke Classics, and a problem stimulated the product development for Partner in Wine.

Case study: Patagonia

The outdoor clothing retailer Patagonia is well-known for its commitment to environmental sustainability and social responsibility. In late 2018, they changed their original mission statement from a product/purpose hybrid of 'Build the best product, cause no unnecessary harm, use business to inspire and implement solutions to the environmental crisis' to the clear purpose-driven mission 'Patagonia is in business to save our home planet.' By emphasizing storytelling and highlighting environmental causes rather than focusing solely on promoting its products, Patagonia prioritizes delivering its environmental message to its followers.

Their Instagram account showcases stunning photos and authentic inspirational stories that resonate with their outdoor lifestyle-focused audience. At first glance, their feed looks like an individual's account who has a huge passion for all things adventure. It takes a few seconds to register that it is a brand account.

On Facebook, Patagonia extends its content strategy by sharing longer videos, links to articles and a wide range of events associated with its brand. They capitalize on the opportunity to create and promote events, tapping into the millennial desire for experiences and fostering a sense of community.

By curating and sharing news and information related to nature, national parks, voting and conservation efforts on X (Twitter), Patagonia strengthens its position as a thought leader in the environmental space and keeps its audience informed and engaged.

Are you clear about why your business exists? Your purpose can be the cornerstone of your narrative and your core values can form another essential element in shaping your business story.

Your storytelling will also focus on your chosen differentiation strategy. You will be bringing your value proposition to life through communication of your brand promise.

Are you clear about why your business exists?

Align this work with your brand identity and you are almost ready. Remember, it's not just about visual identity, but also how you want your business to sound on social media. Whether it's a professional tone, a conversational approach, or a touch of humour, maintaining consistency in your language is also important.

A great example of a brand with a humorous voice on social media is the fast-food restaurant chain, Wendy's. At the time of writing their X (Twitter) bio says *'We like our tweets the way we like our fries: hot, crispy, and better than anyone expects from a fast food restaurant.'* Wendy's personify their brand as cheeky, sassy and confident. They use humour and playful banter to engage with their audience.

By contrast, a brand with a more serious tone is the *New York Times*. Their voice on social media is characterized by professionalism, reliability and credibility. Their commitment to journalistic integrity and factual reporting reflects in the way they communicate with their audience. They maintain a respectful and authoritative tone in their articles and social media posts.

With all these elements in place, you'll be well on your way to creating a captivating business story that deeply connects with your audience.

Let's explore how to put this into practice.

Getting attention

To create a social media post that tells your story effectively, it's essential to start with a captivating hook that immediately grabs your audience's attention. This opening should be engaging, using a surprising fact, thought-provoking question, or a concise, powerful statement. The goal is to pique viewers' interest and encourage them to keep reading or watching.

Social media posts on some platforms have limited space, so it's important to get straight to the point. Carefully choose your words and eliminate any unnecessary details that don't contribute to the core message. Keep in mind that a concise post is more likely to hold your audience's attention.

Visual elements, such as images, videos or graphics that enhance the narrative, are essential in complementing your story. Remember the adage that a picture can speak a thousand words, and choose visuals that align with the story's message and provide context or emotional impact. Visuals play a significant role in capturing your audience's attention, stopping them from scrolling past your content on their screen.

Don't forget that customers' decisions to buy are based on both rationality and emotion. Creating an emotional connection while also providing logical and fact-based information is an effective way to engage your audience in your story. Adding the rational aspect helps your audience understand the practical benefits and value that your products or services offer, ensuring a more well-rounded narrative that appeals to both the heart and the mind.

Decisions to buy are based on both rationality and emotion

Your post should offer a solution to the problem presented, an insight, or a valuable lesson learned. This resolution provides value to your audience and leaves them with a clear takeaway from your story.

Understanding the nuances of content on different social media platforms is essential for effective communication and engagement. Each platform has its unique features, demographics and user behaviours, which influence the type of content that resonates best with its users. For instance, Instagram is primarily visual-centric, with a focus on high-quality images and videos. Captions play a crucial role in providing context or storytelling, but the platform doesn't support clickable links within captions, requiring users to include links in their bio or utilize features like Instagram Stories for linking. Platforms like X (Twitter) prioritize brevity and real-time interaction, with a character limit for posts. LinkedIn, being a professional networking platform, emphasizes thought leadership content, such as articles, industry insights and career-related updates.

The best way to understand platform-specific differences is to actively engage as a user and observe the unique characteristics, user behaviours and content trends first hand. They are always evolving.

Engagement on social media

Once you have your audience's attention, effort should focus on engagement. On social media this refers to the interactions, reactions and responses that users have with your content such as likes, shares, direct messages and clicks through to a website page. Engagement signifies that your content is resonating with your audience. Additionally, **Guide your viewers into thinking, feeling and taking action** engagement often amplifies the reach of your content, because likes, shares and comments can increase the visibility of your posts to a broader audience.

Social media is not just about broadcasting a message; it's about creating a two-way social conversation.

To maximize interactions, guide your viewers into thinking, feeling and taking action. When preparing your post, have 'engagement' in mind. Here's some examples:

- **Inspire thoughts:** Share quotes, statements or facts. Encourage your audience to ponder, reflect or consider a new perspective. By stimulating their thoughts, you increase

97

the likelihood of receiving thoughtful comments and opinions. 'On this day' milestone reflections can work well here, embracing the tried and tested nostalgia approach.

- **Encourage action:** Use strong calls to action (CTAs) that instruct your viewers on what to do next. Whether it's inviting them to like, share, comment, click a link or participate in a poll, clear and compelling CTAs guide your audience to take immediate and specific actions, enhancing overall engagement. You cannot assume that viewers of a social media post will know what to do – even if they are active users, they are often distracted – so a clear reminder is always useful.

- **Encourage sharing:** Create posts that are highly shareable and benefit from being spread within social networks. Shareable content often includes tips, humour, inspirational stories or useful information, as people are more inclined to share posts that they believe will be valuable or entertaining to their friends and followers. I love a recommendation of a TedTalk to watch or book to read.

- **Foster discussion:** Create content that invites discussions and debates. Thought-provoking questions can spur conversations in the comments section, increasing engagement as your audience shares their viewpoints and interacts with one another. This type of content can be both evergreen (not time-specific) or related to current news and trends. Social media platforms such as LinkedIn and X (Twitter) are ideal for identifying current topics.

The importance of content calendars

A content calendar is a valuable tool used in social media marketing to plan and organize content creation and distribution across various platforms. It serves as a roadmap, outlining what content will be shared, when it will be posted, and on which platforms. The calendar is an agile working document as it's likely that trending content will be added in when the opportunity is relevant.

One of the primary benefits of a content calendar is its ability to maintain consistency in posting frequency and content quality. By planning posts in advance, marketers can ensure a steady stream of engaging content that keeps followers interested and informed. This consistency is crucial for building brand awareness, establishing credibility and fostering a loyal audience base.

A content calendar enables marketers to align their social media efforts with broader marketing objectives and campaigns. By mapping out content themes and topics in advance, marketers can ensure that their social media content supports larger marketing initiatives, such as product launches, promotions or seasonal campaigns.

It's all too easy to 'set and forget' if you plan ahead and use a scheduling tool for social media management, but it's vital you stay involved with your social media posts 'in the moment'.

The key to building relationships that will help your business grow is to nurture the engagement on your posts with additional responses – a simple thank you is good; dive deeper into a comment where you can. And remember, this does not all need to be in the public domain. If you can spot an opportunity – I call it a conversation trigger – send a direct message, email or even pick up the phone!

You should also allocate time to engaging with content in your newsfeed, for the companies and individuals you are following. This is all part of 'being social' and building reciprocal relationships.

It's vital you stay involved with your social media posts

Liking, sharing and commenting on posts you see – where you can add value to the author, and to your own audience – is good practice. Also, moving to private direct messages when appropriate will help you to deepen relationships and explore potential opportunities.

Building an online following

Storytelling and engaging content are powerful tools for attracting new followers on social media. Followers who will be at the 'awareness' stage of their decision-making journey.

By consistently delivering content that resonates and telling stories that captivate, businesses and individuals can create a domino effect. Your existing followers engage with your content, increasing its visibility, and in turn, this attracts new followers who are drawn in by the engaging narrative and meaningful interactions.

Building your online following will not 'just happen' through content. Achieving engagement that will extend the reach of your content to new followers is valuable. Using keywords and hashtags will help your content get found by new followers who are seeking content around your topics.

The value of hashtags

The hashtag was popularized on Twitter in 2007 by Chris Messina, who suggested using the symbol to collate groups of related Tweets. Since then, hashtags have become ubiquitous across various social media platforms, including Instagram, Facebook, LinkedIn and TikTok.

Hashtags serve several valuable purposes on social media. Firstly, they facilitate content discovery and engagement by organizing posts around specific topics or themes. Users can search for or click on hashtags to explore related content and participate in discussions or events. Hashtags enable users to join larger conversations, movements or trending topics, amplifying their reach and visibility within the social media community.

By incorporating relevant hashtags into their posts, individuals and businesses can expand their reach beyond their existing followers, attract new followers and drive traffic to their profiles or websites.

Researching relevant hashtags is an important part of the social media management role. It starts with observation and can be supported by tools such as Hashtagify (www .hashtagify.me) and Best Hashtags (www.best-hashtags .com).

You need to actively pursue growth of your accounts; this is an activity often forgotten, because the perception of social media is that it is all about posting content. It also isn't easy. Buying followers is an option, but it is unlikely to be effective as bought followers are rarely real (they are likely to be fake accounts), and bots are never going to do business with you. *Please, do not buy followers!* The best practice approach is to identify your target audience (using your customer personas) and engage with their social media accounts.

When considering how to build your following, you need to keep your target audience in mind and build the *right* following. You can check out your followers using insights tools – these are

Build the *right* following   available natively on Facebook and Instagram. On LinkedIn, a Company Page admin can access demographic insights for page followers. For individual profiles on LinkedIn, you can access demographic insights for those viewing your posts, by company size, job title, location and industry.

For an up-to-date guide to social media analytics, visit www .luanwise.co.uk/books/smart-social-media or scan the QR code below.

Organic vs paid social media content

The choice between organic and paid content has become a key consideration for brands aiming to establish a robust online presence.

Organic content, driven by authentic engagement and user-generated interactions, fosters a genuine connection with the audience. On the other hand, paid content leverages targeted advertising to amplify reach and visibility.

As evidenced by the growth in social media advertising spend, which increased from $189.1 billion in January 2023 to $207.1 billion in January 2024, marking a 9.5 per cent increase (Source: DataReportal), businesses are increasingly recognizing the value of advertising.

Each major platform, including Facebook, Instagram, Twitter, LinkedIn and TikTok, offers self-service tools that streamline the setup and management of advertising campaigns.

These self-service tools provide businesses with the flexibility to create and customize ad campaigns according to their specific goals and objectives. From setting campaign budgets and defining target audiences to uploading creative and tracking performance metrics, these platforms offer a comprehensive suite of features to support advertisers at every stage of the campaign lifecycle.

One of the key advantages of social media advertising is the ability to select objectives that align with different stages of the buying decision process. Whether businesses aim to increase brand awareness, drive consideration or encourage conversions, each platform offers a range of objective options to suit their needs. For example, in the awareness stage, businesses can choose objectives such as 'reach' to introduce their brand to new potential customers. In the consideration stage, businesses can select objectives like 'traffic' or 'engagement' to drive website visits, content views or interactions with their brand. These objectives are focused on nurturing relationships with prospects and guiding them through the decision-making process. Finally, in the conversion stage, businesses can opt for objectives such as 'conversions' or 'sales' to drive specific actions, such as purchases, sign-ups or app installations.

Paid advertising allows businesses to reach a larger audience, target specific demographics or interests, and drive more immediate results in terms of website traffic, leads or sales.

To strike a balance between organic and paid content, businesses need to consider their overall marketing goals, audience demographics and budget constraints. Striking a balance between the two creates what is known as the 'halo effect', a phenomenon where the combination of organic and paid content yields greater results than either approach alone. According to LinkedIn, the halo effect is substantiated by data revealing that Company Page Followers exposed to both organic and paid content are 61 per cent more likely to convert compared to those exclusively exposed to paid content. By integrating organic content to build trust and engagement with the audience and supplementing it with targeted paid advertising to expand reach and drive conversions, businesses can achieve strong results on social media platforms.

Chapter summary

Guiding the buyer's journey with social media content is about recognizing the stages of the decision-making process and aligning your messaging accordingly. Social media serves as a channel that can support all stages of the journey with a combination of storytelling, engagement and a mix of organic content and paid advertising. This requires recognition that use of social media is about far more than creating and posting content to achieve results; it also involves focusing on engagement and building a following.

Chapter 6

Unlocking opportunities through collaborations and partnerships

Establishing collaborations and partnerships, whether with influencers, creators or other businesses, holds immense potential for companies striving to expand their reach and drive growth. Before we dive into the benefits of partnerships and collaborations, I'll offer some definitions. Although the terms are often used interchangeably, collaboration can be defined as a situation whereby individuals or entities work together towards a common goal, each contributing their unique skills and resources, and where each maintains control over their own resources. By contrast, a partnership combines resources, which are managed independently of each party. Collaborations might well develop into partnerships.

In terms of social media collaborations, Buffer (the content management and scheduling tool) defines them as, *'the strategic partnerships between individuals, brands or organizations to co-create content and leverage each other's audiences for mutual benefit'*. Here, the terms partnership and collaboration are more loosely defined, possibly because the resources contributed are more nebulous, comprising time, brand awareness, brand reach, and creative input.

There are many ways in which businesses can come together for mutual benefit, whether it's creating new products, promoting shared values or enhancing customer experiences.

One example is Partner in Wine (whose social media use is analyzed as one of the success stories in Chapter 8). Partner in Wine partnered with wine producer Maison Mirabeau to create an insulated wine bottle the same colour as the Mirabeau rosé wine, branded with both companies' names. This enabled both businesses to create a new product and to draw on each other's reach and target audiences.

The partnership between GoPro and Red Bull is another example. This dynamic pairing brought together GoPro's expertise in capturing extreme sports footage with Red Bull's association with high-energy and adrenaline-fuelled activities. The collaboration led to the creation of exclusive, thrilling content that showcased extreme sports and adventure from unique and often breathtaking perspectives.

Both brands actively shared this content across their social media platforms, capitalizing on the visual appeal and excitement of the videos. The partnership **Choosing the right business partner is a critical decision** extended beyond mere content sharing to collaborative events, contests and behind-the-scenes glimpses. By doing so, they tapped into the interests of their target audience – adventure seekers, sports enthusiasts and adrenaline junkies – and fostered a sense of community around their shared passion for extreme experiences.

Choosing the right business partner is a critical decision that can significantly impact the success and trajectory of a business. Whether aiming to leverage complementary strengths, enter new markets, or enhance product offerings, a well-considered business partnership can unlock mutually beneficial opportunities.

In the rest of this chapter, we will look at the relationship between businesses and individuals, and how they are using social media to support business growth.

Case study: Nike

The book *Shoe Dog* by Phil Knight, co-founder of Nike, serves as an early example of the power of influencers. The book chronicles the journey of Nike from its humble beginnings as Blue Ribbon Sports to becoming a global athletic brand.

In the early days of Nike, Phil Knight used influencers to promote the company's shoes in a number of ways. He sent free shoes to Bill Bowerman and his athletes at the University of Oregon. He also partnered with Steve Prefontaine, one of the most popular and successful runners of his time. In addition, he signed endorsement deals with high-profile athletes. Knight also invited Olympic athletes to visit the Nike factory and meet with their designers to shape the development of new product lines. Finally, he staged publicity events featuring Nike athletes and products.

Knight's use of influencers was successful because he was able to identify and partner with individuals who were respected and admired by his target audience. He also made sure to give his influencers the creative freedom to promote Nike products in a way that was authentic and engaging.

The 2023 film *Air* showcases the true story of Nike signing basketball legend Michael Jordan to create the iconic Air Jordan shoe line.

Influencers and creators

The terms influencers and creators, though often used interchangeably, represent distinct roles in the digital landscape.

The concept of influencers can be traced back to the early days of celebrity endorsements. However, what sets influencers apart is their origin within the digital realm. Unlike traditional celebrities, influencers didn't necessarily rise to prominence through mainstream media; they cultivated their followings organically on platforms like Instagram and TikTok.

In the formative years of social media, influencers were often niche experts or enthusiasts who, by virtue of their passion or expertise, amassed devoted followings. These individuals weren't merely endorsing products; they were curating lifestyles, sharing experiences and fostering a sense of community among their followers. Their influence stemmed from the trust they built with their audience. Recommendations felt personal, like advice from a friend, and this authenticity was the currency that fuelled their impact. Whether it was a beauty guru extolling the virtues of a skincare product or a tech enthusiast showcasing the latest gadgets, the power of influencers lay in their ability to bridge the gap between brands and consumers in a way that felt genuine.

Influencers have established an audience on social media and leverage their social media presence to promote or endorse products or services. Their focus extends beyond creating content to influencing the opinions, decisions and behaviours of their followers, often in connection with specific products, services or lifestyle choices. The term 'influencer' itself implies a power dynamic – a capacity to effect changes and inspire action within a dedicated audience.

Creators, on the other hand, are individuals who generate original and engaging content across various platforms like YouTube, Instagram and TikTok. This role often comes under the remit of an in-house social media manager; however, there is an increasing emergence of freelance content creators who specialize in this area. Their creative output spans various mediums and, for freelancers, is often driven by personal interests, skills and passions.

In 2020, research by Signalfire showed that more than 50 million people worldwide consider themselves to be creators. Of these, 46.7 million categorize themselves as amateurs, with over 2 million counting themselves as professional creators, earning enough from their passion to consider it their full-time income.

While influencers and creators initially occupied distinct realms, the evolution of social media has seen a natural convergence of these roles. Influencers became creators as they ventured into producing more original content and creators became influencers as their audiences grew.

Case study: Gary 'Vee' Vaynerchuk

Gary Vaynerchuk, also known as Gary Vee, is a serial entrepreneur, investor, author and speaker.

He is both a successful content creator and an influencer, with over 13 million followers on Instagram, 3.3 million followers on X (Twitter) and 3.4 million subscribers on YouTube.

In his book *Jab, Jab, Jab, Right Hook*, Vaynerchuk argues that businesses should focus on providing value to their audience on social media, rather than simply trying to sell to them. He likens this approach to a boxer who jabs multiple times to set up a powerful right hook. Social media is a long game. It takes time and effort to build a following and see results on social media. Businesses shouldn't expect to go viral overnight. He also stresses the importance of consistency, interacting with followers and building relationships with them.

He produces a variety of original content, such as daily vlogs, podcasts and educational videos, which are shared across social media. Gary Vee's content is known for being raw, authentic and actionable. He covers a wide range of topics, including business, marketing, personal development and current events.

It's important to note that he does not do this alone; Gary Vee has a team of employees who support his content creation and distribution including videographers, editors, producers and social media managers.

Types of influencer

Influencers are often classified based on the size of their audience and reach.

A **mega influencer** is a social media influencer who has amassed a following in excess of 1 million followers across multiple platforms. Mega influencers are often well-known personalities, celebrities or individuals who have gained significant fame outside social media platforms. They can include actors, musicians, athletes and other public figures. The appeal of mega influencers lies in their widespread recognition, and they often have the potential to reach millions with a single post or endorsement. However, this does of course come with a hefty price tag, and it's worth noting that while mega influencers can provide broad exposure, their followers might not have the same level of personal connection or engagement compared to followers of smaller influencers.

Macro influencers, characterized by followings often in the hundreds of thousands, are typically well-established figures in their niche. They possess the potential to reach a broad audience, making them suitable for extensive brand awareness campaigns. However, collaborating with macro influencers can be relatively expensive, and authenticity may become a concern due to their frequent participation in large-scale marketing efforts.

Mid-tier influencers, boasting follower counts between 50,000 and 500,000, strike a balance between reach and engagement, often cultivating highly interactive and loyal communities. Their follower base is substantial enough to ensure significant visibility, yet still intimate enough to foster personal connections and trust.

On the other hand, **micro influencers**, with more modest followings ranging from 10,000 to 50,000 followers, are often niche experts or enthusiasts. Collaborating with micro influencers is generally more cost-effective than working with mega or macro influencers, and their specialized content resonates deeply with a dedicated and engaged audience, resulting in higher engagement rates.

Nano influencers represent the smallest tier, with audiences ranging from 1,000 to several thousand followers. Often everyday individuals passionate about specific topics, nano influencers offer hyper-local or hyper-niche influence. They foster a more personal and authentic connection with their audience due to their smaller following, making them suitable for location-specific or highly specialized campaigns.

Case study: Francis Bourgeois

Francis Bourgeois is a British trainspotter, social media personality, model and author. He is most known for his lighthearted and humorous videos on the topic of trains, posted to TikTok and Instagram. To date, he has 2 million followers on Instagram.

Bourgeois' success as a social media influencer has helped to raise the profile of trainspotting and make it more accessible to a wider audience. He has also inspired a new generation of trainspotters to take up the hobby. Bourgeois has also used his platform to raise awareness for important causes, such as mental health and autism, and has spoken out about the importance of diversity and inclusion in the rail industry.

Bourgeois' popularity has made him a sought-after influencer for brands. He has worked with a variety of brands, from British Rail, National Rail, Crossrail, Transport for London, Great Western Railway, Virgin Trains and Hornby.

In 2022, Bourgeois appeared in a campaign video for a collaboration between The North Face and Gucci, branded as The North Face x Gucci. The video was shot at a railway station in the Alps and showcased the collection's outdoor-inspired ready-to-wear pieces. Bourgeois' authenticity and passion for trains made him a perfect fit for the collaboration, and his fans were excited to see him represent The North Face x Gucci. The collaboration also benefited Bourgeois, as it gave him the opportunity to work with two of the world's most prestigious brands and reach a wider audience. It also helped to confirm his status as one of the most popular and influential trainspotters in the world.

The choice of influencer will depend on many factors. Table 6.1 below summarizes the influencer types, the budgets that might be required to work with them and the stage of the buyer's journey where the collaboration is likely to be most effective.

TABLE 6.1: TYPES OF INFLUENCER

Influencer type	Follower numbers	Description	Budget	Relevant stage of the buyer's journey
Mega influencer	Over 1 million	Individuals with global reach, suitable for major campaigns targeting a wide audience.	Significant budget required	Awareness
Macro influencer	500,000 to 1 million	Individuals who are well-known in their field, offering broad reach for brands.	Large budget required	Awareness
Mid-tier influencer	50,000 to 500,000	Individuals who have a dedicated and engaged following, offering a balance of reach and intimacy for brands	Medium budget required	Interest and Desire
Micro influencer	10,000 to 50,000	Niche experts with high audience engagement, ideal for reaching a targeted audience and fostering relationships with potential customers.	Medium–small budget required	Interest and Desire
Nano influencer	1,000 to 10,000	Despite fewer followers, nano influencers often have highly engaged audiences focused on niche topics.	Minimal budget required; possible exchange of products only.	Loyalty

Working with influencers and creators

There are many ways to find relevant influencers and creators to work with. You could simply use the search bar on a social media platform to search for keywords related to your industry or target audience. You can also browse through popular hashtags to find creators who are posting about relevant topics.

Some platforms have specific features such as TikTok's Creator Marketplace (https://creatormarketplace.tiktok.com/) or YouTube's BrandConnect (https://www.youtube.com/ads/brandconnect/) which help you to search for and identify influencers in your niche.

There are also a number of third-party tools that allow you to search and connect with influencers and creators. For example BuzzSumo (https://buzzsumo.com), Glewee (https://glewee.com), HypeAuditor (https://www.hypeauditor.com), Klear (https://explore.klear.com), Traackr (https://www.traackr.com) and Upfluence (https://get.upfluence.com).

It is important to do detailed research to make sure that there is an alignment of target audiences and values. An influencer might, at first glance, seem to be a perfect fit, but you should take time to explore what other projects they're working on or have in development, and whether they will be in competition with the collaboration you have in mind. Check whether they routinely comment on political or ethical issues for example, and whether these are in alignment with your brand. If your brand is resolutely politically neutral, you might be better off working with a different influencer. Importantly, check what posts and comments the influencer has made in the past, to ensure they align fully with your purpose and values. Values that are in tune with the values held by both your business and your target audience will make your collaboration more authentic, and from authenticity comes trust.

Here's some advice from Head of Strategic Partnerships at Agorapulse and Fractional CMO, Mike Allton:

'Understanding a potential influencer's worldview and alignment with your brand are critical before proceeding, which is why I recommend that you personally take the time to read some of their posts, comment on them, and engage with that influencer. If you rely solely on reports and metrics, you cannot hope to get an understanding of what this person is like and whether or not they're the kind of influencer that you'd want to work with and have representing your brand.

This is also an opportunity for you to gauge how they react to and respond to their audience – which are the folks you hope will soon be your audience. Are they responding to every comment, or ignoring their audience? What's the tone and style of those responses? If the influencer was responding as you, as your brand, to one of those comments, how comfortable would you be?

It's a little more time up front, but this engagement will help you to foster a stronger relationship with a potential influencer or brand ambassador who goes beyond paid campaigns because there is deep alignment and a strong relationship in place.'

Authenticity and trust

Authenticity and trust stand as foundational pillars for the success of collaborations with influencers, creators and brand ambassadors.

When people trust and believe in the influencers and creators they follow, they are more likely to be influenced by their recommendations and purchase the products and services they promote. However, consumers are becoming increasingly sophisticated and able to spot inauthentic endorsements. When

Authenticity and trust stand as foundational pillars

creators and influencers promote products and services that they don't actually use or believe in, it is clear to their followers.

In her book *Who Can You Trust?*, Rachel Botsman argues that the digital era has ushered in a new paradigm where trust is shifting from traditional institutions to distributed networks facilitated by technology. For example, every day people are now renting their homes to strangers on AirBnB and getting in the car of an unknown Uber driver.

In the context of social media, Botsman argues that these platforms have become central to how individuals establish and maintain trust. People increasingly rely on online reviews, recommendations and social connections to make decisions, from purchasing products to forming opinions about political candidates.

Social media's reputation has long been tarnished by a myriad of issues ranging from misinformation and disinformation to concerns about transparency, cyberbullying and child safety. However, in 2023, in the context of increased regulation and tightened content moderation, the social media sector saw the first rise in trustworthiness since its inclusion in the Ipsos Trustworthiness Monitor. The UK's Online Safety Act of 2023 brought in what is being seen as a new era for Internet safety as legislation allows children and adults more control over the content they see online, and for stronger action to be taken against online harm. In the US, at the time of writing, online safety legislation that aims to hold social media companies accountable for material posted on their platforms is going through Congress.

Amidst these challenges posed by social media, including its impact on our daily lives much like the once-feared excesses of television viewing, it's evident that governments are a little behind in addressing the impact of emerging technologies such as social media and AI. However, we are all navigating the complexities together and must take responsibility to evaluate the information and connections encountered on social media, to mitigate risks and leverage the potential of these platforms in our increasingly interconnected world.

Case study: #TikTokMadeMeBuyIt

Word-of-mouth marketing goes far on TikTok. When creators share product reviews that are genuine and entertaining, people pay attention. It's effective because TikTok's reputation for videos where people can be truly themselves, lends authenticity to their voices. This shift towards the 'homespun' occurred during the Covid-19 lockdown, when influencers and brands were less able to produce polished, well-produced videos, and videos often included domestic backgrounds, family and pet intrusions, and bloopers.

The #TikTokMadeMeBuyIt hashtag has many success stories in which brands have seen successful social commerce conversions, from both paid influencers and regular users.

A 2021 study by Nielsen shows that users find TikTok content more authentic than other platforms. The study also shows TikTok as a place where users feel free to be themselves.

An average of 64 per cent of TikTok users say they can be their true selves on TikTok, while an average of 56 per cent of TikTok users say they can post videos they wouldn't post elsewhere. This sentiment isn't limited to a particular location, language or culture. According to the study, users in Canada, Brazil, Indonesia and Russia all feel equally comfortable about being themselves on TikTok. An average of 53 per cent of TikTok users say they trust others to be their real selves on TikTok too.

Once you have identified a business, influencer or creator that you would like to work with, you can reach out to them directly via social media or email to start a conversation.

Once you've established how you will work together, you must then turn to drawing up a contract of expectations, setting out clearly what you expect the influencer to do, and when. These guidelines should also include any regulations about your products / services (some industry sectors are subject to guidance) and also adherence to legal regulation. In the UK, advertising is covered by ASA, the Advertising Standards Agency. The UK code of non-broadcast advertising and direct & promotional marketing (the CAP code) applies to all advertising, including paid promotions and content created by influencers on social media. One aspect of adhering to the advertising rules is that influencers must explicitly state when their content includes paid advertising or sponsorship. It must be clear to social media users that the social media post they're viewing is advertising, often by using the hashtag #ad.

There are many examples of success with collaborations and partnerships. However, sometimes things can go wrong. The following case study highlights how working with an influencer can go wrong if you fail to prepare adequately both for the reaction to the collaboration itself, and to the results.

Case study: Dylan Mulvaney and Bud Light

Dylan Mulvaney is a transgender social media influencer and activist. She is known for her entertaining and informative videos about transgender identity and her own experiences transitioning. Dylan has a large following on TikTok and Instagram, where she regularly shares her thoughts and feelings on a variety of topics, including gender, sexuality and body positivity.

Dylan has collaborated with a number of brands, including American Eagle, Amazon, Kate Spade, MAC Cosmetics and Fenty Beauty.

In April 2023, Dylan collaborated with Bud Light to promote their 'Easy Carry Contest'. The campaign invited participants to showcase their strength by carrying as many beer cans as possible, for a chance to win $15,000. Dylan appeared in a sponsored video wearing an Audrey Hepburn-inspired outfit and playfully referencing March Madness (the US college basketball tournament). Additionally, Bud Light released a line of Pride-themed cans with different pronouns to celebrate Dylan's first anniversary since transitioning.

However, the venture was met with backlash from some customers, who called for a boycott of the beer brand. Sales also began to decline. When things started to go wrong, the company's response to the boycott was widely criticized as being inadequate.

Anheuser-Busch InBev, the parent company of Bud Light, eventually pulled the ad campaign. Dylan Mulvaney shared her thoughts in a candid TikTok video, expressing her dissociation from the hate and cruelty thrown her way, and calling for more inclusivity in brand partnerships.

Being prepared for a potential crisis, and knowing how to handle a situation if it arises, is an essential part of business risk management. This involves closely monitoring social media channels for any signs of brewing crises, such as customer complaints or negative sentiment about a brand. In readiness there should be clearly defined roles and responsibilities, pre-approved message templates and escalation procedures. It's always key to pause any scheduled social media posts and to review the situation in real-time before returning to business-as-usual.

For more details on balancing the benefits and risks of social media, see my previous book *Planning for Success: A practical guide to setting and achieving your social media marketing goals.*

User-generated content

While collaborating with influencers and creators can undoubtedly amplify your brand's reach and engagement, it's essential not to overlook the invaluable contribution of your customers.

User-Generated Content (UGC) posted by customers is often perceived to be more relatable and authentic. An added benefit is that it's usually freely available for a business to access and amplify UGC via their own accounts, and the customer loves that they have been recognized and celebrated. Hashtags can serve as valuable signposts to identifying UGC and can be used to encourage customers to create and share content using a branded hashtag.

An excellent example of UGC in action is Spotify Wrapped, an annual event since 2016 where Spotify users receive personalized insights into their listening habits over the past year. Through a combination of data analytics and engaging visuals, Spotify Wrapped presents users with their top songs, artists, genres and listening trends. Users share their Spotify Wrapped summaries on social media, sparking discussions, comparisons and recommendations based on their music preferences. This user-generated buzz not only fosters a sense of community among Spotify users but also serves as free promotion for the platform. In 2022 over 156 million users engaged with Spotify Wrapped.

It's essential not to overlook the invaluable contribution of your customers

---

Chapter summary

Seizing opportunities through strategic collaborations and partnerships is hugely valuable for businesses aiming to expand their reach and drive growth.

These alliances, whether with influencers, creators or other brands, offer a myriad of advantages. However, selecting the right collaborator is paramount. Whether engaging mega influencers, macro influencers, micro influencers or nano influencers, aligning values and target audiences is imperative. Moreover, authenticity and trust are non-negotiable in influencer partnerships, as today's consumers demand genuine recommendations and transparent endorsements.

In navigating the landscape of social media collaborations, businesses must also be equipped to address potential challenges and crises. Proactive monitoring of social channels, clear communication protocols and swift response strategies are critical components of effective risk management. By striking a delicate balance between the opportunities and risks inherent in social media collaborations, businesses can harness the full potential of these partnerships to drive growth and foster meaningful connections with their audience.

Chapter 7

The power of community for business growth

Establishing a robust following or network of connections on social media is indeed a significant achievement, but it marks just the initial phase of leveraging these platforms for business growth. The real power lies in converting followers or connections into tangible opportunities.

Unlike traditional marketing media such as television advertising, out-of-home posters or direct mail through your letterbox, social media provides the opportunity for two-way communication. This requires a mindset that social media is not simply about creating and posting content (broadcasting) and that it is 'social'! Being social thrives on dialogue and interaction. While one-to-one relationships can be built through following/connecting, commenting on posts and private direct messaging, communities can serve as a natural progression for social media users looking to build more meaningful relationships and engage more authentically, with more people.

Social media provides the opportunity for two-way communication

For the social media platforms, investment in community features, such as Groups, support their own growth goals for user acquisition and retention; communities generate valuable content and discussions, providing individuals with a reason to return and spend more time on the platform.

Facebook began to shift its emphasis away from the newsfeed and towards groups following the 2016 US presidential election. At the time, the company was under fire for not doing more to prevent the spread of fake news and misinformation. As part of its response, Facebook CEO Mark Zuckerberg published a 6,000-word note in February 2017 outlining how the social network would improve by focusing on supporting and creating safe communities. Today, Meta has around 40,000 people working on safety and security and it reports on Community Standards Enforcement matters on a quarterly basis.

Community vs Following

Before we go further into communities and how they work, let's establish exactly what we mean by a social media community, and how it differs from a 'following':

Lucy Hall, Founder of *Digital Women* – a community for empowering women in the digital age – regularly comments on the difference between a following and a community. *'People often use the word "community," but what they really have is an audience. A community is NOT just people following someone or a brand. A community is about people coming together, whether many or few. It's a group with shared interests, problems or goals, fostering a space where they all belong.'*

Broadly speaking, followers react to material posted by the brand they follow, whereas members of communities create and react to their own content. Community involvement is about more than a social media presence or lurking in a group to 'listen'. Community members are active, supportive and highly engaged in dialogue.

When we actively participate in communities, we can reap rewards through taking our connections to a deeper relationship level and foster wider networks that can work together for common good.

As individuals, we possess an innate need for belonging and a desire to connect and share experiences with like-minded souls.

Social media communities have the capability to support this human need for belonging by creating an atmosphere where individuals feel secure, accepted and free to express themselves without fear of judgement – a concept commonly known as psychological safety.

We possess an innate need for belonging

In psychologically safe online communities, individuals are more likely to actively participate, feeling that their contributions are valued and that they belong to a supportive group. This fosters an environment where users can be authentic, contributing to a richer and more meaningful exchange of ideas. Ultimately, psychological safety enhances the quality of online interactions and community engagement.

Trust is key to a safe and successful online community

Trust is key to a safe and successful online community. One way to create the safe place is by establishing clear community guidelines that outline the expectations for content and commenting. Communities often require moderating to ensure that guidelines are being followed and to address any issue that may arise.

When trust is created, it leads to increased engagement, growth and loyalty.

Research by Keller Advisory Group (2022) highlighted that the communities people belong to or browse online are deemed trustworthy when it comes to products or brands to buy, according to 68 per cent of consumers (19 per cent trust them 'a lot' and 49 per cent 'some'). Consumers aged 18–24 are the most likely to trust online communities 'a lot'.

Case study: Scamp & Dude

Scamp & Dude is a fashion brand with a deeply personal origin story. Jo Tutchener-Sharp, the founder, faced a serious health crisis when she suffered a brain haemorrhage in 2015. As she was recovering from brain surgery, she missed her two young children, and wished for something to comfort them while she was in hospital. She created the 'Superhero Sleep Buddy', a comforter with a pocket on the back to hold a photo of your child's special person to watch over them, even when they're apart. For every Superhero Sleep Buddy sold, another is donated to a child who has lost a parent, or who is seriously ill themselves.

Expanding into womenswear, the brand's signature design features vibrant colours and a distinctive Superhero lightning bolt motif, symbolizing strength and empowerment. Scamp & Dude also have a #SuperScarfMission to support women starting chemotherapy. For every 'Super Scarf' product sold, another is donated to a woman with cancer.

The 'Scamp & Duders' Facebook Group, with over 12,000 members, was set up as a safe social space for interacting and offering helpful tips and support when needed. Its community members have created new friendships and daily conversations are focused on the launch of new items for sale, visits to stores, sharing new purchases and spotting a 'Duder' in the wild wearing the brand.

Find out more about Scamp and Dude at www .scampanddude.com

Social media communities

Social media presents a diverse range of communities, spanning from lively and interactive discussions within Facebook Groups and professional networking on platforms like LinkedIn, to the multifaceted forums on Reddit, and the live streaming and gaming communities on platforms like Twitch.

Some communities are formed by brands, often to support their customers in some way, as in the Scamp & Dude case study above, or to focus on a social issue that the brand champions. Here, although the focus is on the members of the group, it is still largely brand led. By contrast, interest groups can be formed by anyone on the social media platform. They're not tied to a brand and members share a particular experience, profession, interest or concern.

On Facebook you are likely to find communities (groups) focused on interests, from cleaning to cooking, from photography to property renovation.

Groups on Facebook can be public or private. Public groups are visible to anyone to search and join, while private (hidden) groups require an invitation. Facebook Groups offer various features, from the ability to post text, images, video and links through to file sharing and events.

In the Chapter 8 case study for The VA Handbook, you can learn more about how Facebook Groups have helped not only to sell products but also acted as a way to support individuals in their own business growth by becoming a safe and nurturing space for members to share problems and advice.

LinkedIn Groups are primarily focused on professional networking and industry-related discussion. Like Facebook Groups, LinkedIn Groups can be public or private. They require approval or an invitation to join, and group managers have control over membership.

Case study: The Social C-Suite LinkedIn Group

Damian Corbet established the LinkedIn Group, The Social C-Suite, in 2014 as a place to discuss how leaders can make use of social media. It's a niche community with around 2,500 members exchanging ideas, insights and best practices. As manager of the group, Damian regularly shares relevant articles and observations, encouraging group members to engage in discussions.

The group is set up as a public group (searchable and open for anyone on LinkedIn to see posts) and has set rules for the group to keep the content focused, relevant and non-commercial. This is, Damian believes, important in ensuring that members of the group find it valuable and a safe place to ask questions, share experiences and most importantly, make new connections.

You can find the group at: https://www.linkedin.com/groups/7473704/

Let's explore the opportunities for individuals, as part of their business role, to participate in communities, then turn to the opportunity for businesses to build and lead a community.

For individuals...

Social media communities bring numerous advantages for individuals as part of their business role. Platforms facilitate connections with like-minded professionals including industry peers and potential mentors, paving the way for collaborations and career advancements. Some of the ways in which communities might support you professionally are:

- **Seeking information** – many join communities to gather information, seek advice and gain knowledge related to their interests or needs.
- **Sharing experiences** – individuals often want to share their experiences, whether it's a success story, or a product review.
- **Networking and connections** – professionals use communities to network, connect with peers and explore career opportunities.
- **Emotional support** – support communities offer a safe space for individuals to discuss personal challenges and find emotional support from others facing similar situations.

Social media communities can also contribute to professional development by sharing industry trends and training course recommendations. Job opportunities are often shared within communities, enabling individuals to explore potential career paths, find job leads and discover freelance opportunities.

Within relevant communities, individuals can participate in discussions to offer advice and insights to other group members. In turn, this helps to position themselves as a subject-matter expert and go-to person on a particular topic. Participating in communities in this way, demonstrating your expertise and helping others, is part of personal branding, and leads to social selling.

In *Social Selling*, author Tim Hughes reminds us that social media platforms are trusted sources of recommendations, and communities on social media are *'now the de facto place to live, work and sell online'*.

Social selling is the strategic use of social media platforms to build relationships, engage with potential customers and provide valuable content, as opposed to simply using social media for direct sales pitches or transactions.

The efficacy of building a personal brand and social selling is also highlighted in *Belonging to the Brand: Why Community is the Last Great Marketing Strategy*, where author Mark Schaefer says, *'Today's consumers will block you, ban you, and run away from you if they sense you're trying to manipulate them with your marketing. Instead of sell, sell, sell, you need to help, help, help.'* Being a valuable member of online communities helps you to achieve this.

For businesses...

Management consulting firm McKinsey & Company declared 'community' as the next big idea in marketing for the 2020s. A key contributing factor to this approach is the ever-increasing noise and challenge of capturing attention using traditional marketing tactics that are also getting stale and expensive.

So how can businesses use communities for marketing?

In their best practice guide to Community Based Marketing, Ashley Friedlein and Michelle Goodall offer the definition, *'Community Based Marketing (CBM) is bringing people together around a shared practice, purpose, place, product or set of circumstances to create insights and closer, more valuable relationships with prospects, customers and other stakeholders to deliver organizational value.'*

Businesses can leverage community-based marketing by actively participating and engaging within relevant online forums, groups and social media communities

Businesses can leverage community-based marketing

where their target audience congregates. By becoming valuable contributors to these communities, companies can establish themselves as trusted authorities and build rapport with potential customers.

Another effective approach, as we have already seen, is to create branded communities where customers can connect with each other, share experiences and provide feedback. These communities serve as valuable platforms for brand advocacy, product discussions and customer support. By facilitating these interactions, the brand not only strengthens customer loyalty but also gains valuable insights into customer preferences and behaviours, which can inform future marketing initiatives and product development efforts. There are many platforms available for community building, including Facebook and LinkedIn plus niche platforms such as Slack and Discord.

Let's take a look at another community example...

Case Study: Crocs

Crocs are a comfortable, brightly coloured, moulded-foam clog, so named because from the side they resemble a crocodile's snout. They were launched in 2002 and enjoyed immediate success with boaters, gardeners, healthcare workers and children, and anyone who wanted shoes that were easy to clean and comfortable to wear. The success of the brand grew rapidly, with global sales of Crocs increasing from $1.2 million in 2003 to $850 million by 2007.

The ugliness of the original Crocs had always been polarizing – people either loved them or hated them. The clogs' appearance attracted increasing criticism and, coupled with the global economic downturn in 2008, Crocs' stock price plummeted. The situation worsened in the 2010s, with numerous social media memes mercilessly mocking the shoe for its ugliness. The problem was not that no one was aware of the brand – the memes meant that consumers easily recognized the clogs – but that consumers no longer wanted to own them.

To turn their fortunes around, the team at Crocs embraced the shoe's iconic ugliness, using a series of campaigns that didn't aim to convert those who disliked the shoe but to celebrate the Crocs community who loved it. Using hashtags such as #findyourfun, customers were encouraged to post pictures of their Crocs on social media. Another campaign invited Crocs wearers to share what made them personally one-of-a-kind, just like the shoes themselves.

Crocs leaned into its fans by launching the #ThousandDollarCrocs challenge on TikTok, inviting followers to post what they thought a $1,000 pair of Crocs would look like. This generated 45,000 videos from the community and an additional 100,000 followers within a week. Crocs also reacted quickly to community-generated trends, for example by establishing 'Croctober' after Crocs fans had adopted National Crocodile Day on X (Twitter) to express their love of Crocs shoes rather than the animal.

By listening in to their community, responding rapidly and celebrating the uniqueness of their fans, Crocs turned the company around. By 2022 Crocs' global net revenue was $3.6 billion and the brand's iconic ugliness had become cool, worn by celebrities and spotted on fashion catwalks.

Chapter summary

The power of community for business growth yields several key takeaways. Firstly, businesses must recognize the significance of authentic engagement within social media communities, fostering two-way communication and building trust. Secondly, branded communities offer a valuable platform for strengthening customer loyalty, advocacy and gaining insights.

Collaborating with influencers aligned with brand values can further amplify marketing efforts. Creating psychologically safe environments within communities is crucial for fostering active participation and trust.

Individuals can leverage social media communities for networking, professional development and personal branding. By authentically engaging and demonstrating expertise, they can drive social selling strategies and enhance career opportunities. Additionally, businesses can leverage community-based marketing to deliver organizational value and drive growth by actively engaging with relevant online forums and groups.

Chapter 8

Success stories

In the previous chapters, we have explored different aspects of social media marketing including how to build trust, create a community, develop a brand following, and collaborations. For this chapter I interviewed a range of B2B and B2C businesses and am delighted to share their stories of using social media to grow their businesses.

Partner in Wine

www.partnerinwine.co.uk

Background

Partner in Wine began during the 2020 Covid-19 lockdown in response to a problem experienced by its founder, Lucy Hitchcock. Wanting to enjoy the warm, sunny weather by sharing a socially distanced drink in the park with her best friend, Lucy realized that her favourite rosé wine would be warm by the time she got there. A wine sleeve was both ugly and ineffective: once it was unzipped, warm air entered and heated the bottle of wine, and it necessitated both taking a corkscrew to open the wine and carrying the empty bottle back home, as there were no recycling bins at the park. Lucy realized that others must be experiencing the same frustrations and set to work to design an aesthetically pleasing insulated wine bottle that holds a full bottle of wine.

She launched the product in July 2020. Despite having only 300 followers on Instagram at the time, sales of the wine bottle almost recouped her initial investment in the business within days. To support sales and using her experience of working in digital marketing, Lucy researched and identified wine education as a gap of information that she could fill. With this approach to social media content, sales began to surge. And then, in March 2021, a post on TikTok went viral.

Sales rocketed and stocks were exhausted, overnight. With over half a million views in just 12 hours, orders increased by over 1,700 per cent compared to the previous day, with an item selling every two minutes, resulting in a record five-figure sales day. The viral video also brought an additional 15,000 followers on TikTok and 12,000 new followers on Instagram. Luckily, Lucy had moved to using a fulfilment centre a few months before the viral video.

Not long after the TikTok post, Partner in Wine was approached by Selfridges to stock the wine bottle, with a number of other high-street shops including Liberty London, Oliver Bonas and Urban Outfitters following suit. Partner in Wine has also appeared on BBC News, *This Morning*, Mail Online and many other major media platforms.

Lucy has also successfully partnered with wine producer Maison Mirabeau to create an insulated wine bottle the same colour as the Mirabeau rosé wine.

Recognizing that the wine bottle was typically a one-time purchase, new products were developed, again in response to problems that Lucy had personally experienced, and which she understood would be shared by many. These include a picnic blanket with features such as a secure pocket, the ability to peg it down, being capacious enough to fit all your friends, and an insulated iced coffee cup aimed at her numerous followers who don't drink wine.

Use of social media

Partner in Wine focuses on using two social media platforms: Instagram and TikTok. Initially, posts were predominantly static images, but evolved to be almost exclusively video in which Lucy explains the origin of her business, discusses different wines and offers problem solving solutions to her followers.

The emphasis on video is made easier by Lucy's decision when she founded Partner in Wine, to film every aspect of her business and business journey, recording herself as she develops each project, including unboxing deliveries and behind-the-scenes moments. This provides a library of material on which to draw, all of it genuine and showing her unrehearsed reaction to wines, materials and products. This authenticity resonates well with followers, who feel that they know her, empathize with her story and want to see her succeed.

Little of the content posted relates to Partner in Wine products unless it is to promote the launch of a new product. Instead, content focuses on entertaining and educational material about wine – for example, pairing with different flavoured crisps! User-generated content also features, with a trend emerging whereby followers rearrange shop shelves stocking Partner in Wine products, and post before and after photographs of the shelf, which are then reposted on the Partner in Wine accounts. The content posting schedule is simple: two wine-related videos a week and the rest of the content ad hoc or user-generated.

In terms of communities and groups, Partner in Wine has an email list (but no communities or groups on social media), which gives followers advance notice of which wines are about to be featured on TikTok and Instagram. As wines that have been featured by Partner in Wine have subsequently sold out for months, this gives people on the mailing list advance warning of which wines to buy.

After testing the use of paid social, Lucy Hitchcock has concluded that organic growth worked better for her business. She creates all her social media content herself. She is the face of the business, talking directly to her followers, relating her story and letting followers feel that they know her personally.

Analysis

Partner in Wine's social media marketing success is down to three linked factors: a compelling founder story, building a brand identity and focusing on education and entertainment.

That Partner in Wine was founded to solve a common problem gives its story a strength and simplicity; that it occurred during the Covid lockdown and features the restrictions of the time (socially distanced meet-ups) adds to its charm. Though many would argue that launching with only 300 Instagram followers would be challenging, it worked because those followers were engaged and committed to the success of the venture, having followed every step of its development on social media. It is far better to have 300 dedicated followers than 10,000 disinterested ones. The compelling nature of the founding story is such that followers pass it on, word for word, to their friends, leading to greater engagement and brand reach.

That followers continue to be engaged and committed is attributable to Lucy's decision when creating the business not to simply create and sell products, but to build a clear brand, with values such as eschewing plastic, a focus on aesthetics, solving problems experienced by many, and a commitment to providing education about wine. Lucy adheres to these brand values in her content, providing entertaining and educational videos that spark conversations rather than simply promoting products.

The brand identity is also strongly identified with Lucy herself. As the face of the business and letting her personality shine out on video, followers feel that they know and like her, and are committed to her success. Her videos resonate because she doesn't play a part on camera – her reactions are genuine. She describes this as her 'superpower': being the face of a small business makes her engagements with followers more intimate and ultimately more committed. As the adage states, people do business with people.

Evoke Classics

www.evoke-classics.com

Background

Following the end of Series 4 of the fly on the wall TV series *Bangers and Cash*, in which old cars are restored and sold on, Sarah Crabtree posted that she would be leaving the programme. She was soon contacted by Evoke Classics. Together they decided to launch a female-led classic car auction website and community platform.

Beginning from scratch with a tiny existing digital presence, the project established ambitious goals to use Sarah Crabtree's fan base to attract an audience to the Evoke Classics auction site, using Sarah as the face of the Evoke Classics brand. Commencing the project in August 2021 gave marketing agency Nerd Digital, who were tasked with developing the brand, five months in which to generate leads and grow an audience ready for the planned launch of the auction website in December 2021. They used a range of marketing techniques: researching the size of the market; establishing which social media platforms potential customers already used; drawing on industry benchmarks to determine how many website visits, leads and social media engagements would be needed each month; and undertaking split testing to refine and perfect their copy, images and calls to action.

Research indicated that, despite the coronavirus pandemic and downturn in the economy, the classic car market remained buoyant, with the highest earners in the UK seeing an increase in their incomes and classic cars being regarded not only as desirable collector's items but as safe investments. A Statista report into the size of the classic car market in the UK indicated that it was expected to grow to £1.33 billion in 2023. Further, research undertaken by the Federation of British Historic Vehicle Clubs in 2019 found that there were 1.2 million owners of classic cars in the UK, with 9.8 million people expressing an interest in classic cars and 5.1 million people nurturing ambitions of owning one.

By examining potential audiences on Facebook, the team discovered that there was an audience of 1.8 million people in the UK on the platform who were interested in classic cars. As there was an established audience of classic car enthusiasts on Facebook, it was decided to use that platform to build Sarah's fan base further and to build a dedicated Evoke Classics page. They also invested in paid Facebook adverts, targeted at specific demographics, which were identified using research, and where the cost to acquire each lead had been carefully calculated.

The team also created a weekly newsletter giving subscribers news about what is happening in the world of classic cars, and details of events that Sarah will be attending. A YouTube channel features vehicles for sale and shares details of Sarah's own classic car, Ivan, a Russet Brown 1980 Morris Ital 1.3HL.

As a result, (as at January 2024) Sarah Crabtree's fan group on Facebook has over 25,000 members, she has nearly 16,000 followers on X (Twitter) and her YouTube page has over 10,000 subscribers. The Evoke Classics website receives over 70,000 monthly visits, with 20,000 of those from organic search; its Facebook page has 9,000 likes and 12,000 followers; and it has built a community of 30,000 classic car enthusiasts.

This successful marketing strategy has recently been acknowledged by their winning a CIM 2023 Marketing Excellence Award in the best new product or service category.

Use of social media

Engagement with social media has been instrumental at several key moments in the development and success of Evoke Classics: from Sarah posting about her departure following the filming of Series 4, and receiving a message from Evoke Classics to moot their idea about an online classic car auction site; marketing agency Nerd Digital learned about the opportunity with Evoke Classics on LinkedIn; and tapping into the Facebook community of classic car enthusiasts was critical to the success of the venture.

From the outset, Evoke Classics has been clear about the role it wanted social media to play and how each platform will complement each other. Social media is used to drive traffic to the website: the success of this is indicated by analytics that show website visits drop when they post less on social media. Having plenty of content to post is key: Sarah attends numerous classic car events, taking photographs at each one, which she then posts on the Evoke Classics social media accounts.

Each social media platform has a different role to play, with Facebook as the main platform to promote vehicles for sale and to generate leads using lead forms, and X (Twitter) used only for organic content. Further, Sarah made a personal commitment to be more active on social media, prompted by seeing people talking about her on X (Twitter).

Analysis

The key factors that have led to the early success of Evoke Classics are market research and having Sarah Crabtree as the face of the brand.

The research undertaken was extensive, not only to determine the size and value of the market but also to produce high-quality demographic data on high-value potential customers, which in turn, was used to focus paid advertising on Facebook. Continuing to test and measure the effectiveness of every aspect of each marketing campaign has enabled Evoke Classics to perfect their messaging, tone and imagery. This has resulted in above-average growth such that they can scale back paid advertising as the business is growing organically.

Growth can also be attributed to having Sarah Crabtree as the face of the brand, and by putting effort into growing her personal brand alongside that of Evoke Classics. Despite the industry being male-dominated, having a female face of the brand has not been detrimental: 89.5 per cent of people on the mailing list are men, suggesting that establishing Sarah's credibility on classic cars has succeeded in overcoming stereotypical norms. That she uses social media widely to document the events she attends and how she is restoring her own vintage vehicle both boosts her credibility and also offers a story that followers can engage with. Sarah's founder story and personal brand is easy to understand and get behind, and underlines the brand's stated values of challenging the masculine status quo and building a community of classic car enthusiasts.

The VA Handbook

www.thevahandbook.com

Background

The VA Handbook provides online courses and a paid membership to assist people who want to set up a virtual assistant business. A virtual assistant, or VA, can be defined as a freelancer who typically helps small businesses or consultants with tasks they're unable to do or dislike, or where it makes financial sense to outsource the work. Although traditionally virtual assistants came from administrative or office-based backgrounds, increasingly they now have technical or IT-based skills.

The VA Handbook was created by Joanne Munro, herself a VA since 2008, when she was looking to create a passive income stream and realized that the question she was most asked was 'how to set up as a VA'. In May 2014 she created the VA Handbook website and in August an inexpensive downloadable guide showing people how to set up their own VA business. In early 2015 Jo started to offer 1:1 client training. This later led to the creation of an online course addressing the questions she was typically asked by her 1:1 clients (the course eventually replaced the 1:1 sessions completely).

In 2016, Jo created a VA Handbook Facebook community group, which currently has over 22,500 members and grows by 300 new members every month. She now operates three Facebook groups: the VA Handbook Group, a private group for established Virtual Assistants called The Rockstars, for those who have purchased her flagship online course, and a paid-for membership group called the VA All Stars. All three groups are very active, with a team of moderators around the world moderating posts 24/7.

From inception, Jo has been clear about the purpose of her business and how each strand of her marketing cross-pollinates the others. She has four calls to action she encourages her audience to make: download the free resources from her website, sign up to her email list, read her blog posts, and join the Facebook group. Each channel feeds the others: the website and newsletter mention the Facebook groups; the Facebook group leads back to the website, the free downloads and the email newsletter.

One of her brand values is to post useful, valuable and authentic material, with a commitment to getting straight to the point and not sugar-coating issues, an approach that resonates well with her audience. It won her the VA Voice Best VA Training Provider for 2023.

She uses an evergreen social media scheduler, creating and repurposing evergreen content and updating images and content regularly.

After experimenting with paid social, her metrics told her that most of her customers were reaching her organically, through mentions of her business in other Facebook groups, and through referrals. Consequently, she now focuses her marketing effort on organic posts on Facebook and LinkedIn, website SEO, an email newsletter, plus building the Facebook group communities.

Use of social media

Jo's use of social media has changed over time as the platforms themselves have changed and she herself has found less time to spend on social media. After experimenting with most of the platforms except TikTok (which isn't currently used by her customer demographic), and after carefully measuring where her leads were coming from, she has focused on Facebook and LinkedIn. She trials new features on Facebook when they emerge, again testing and measuring and only keeping the ones that work for her, her business and her group members. In particular, she notes that the Guides section, where resources can be stored under different headings, is useful to direct members to information. On LinkedIn, Jo regularly shares content including a version of her weekly email newsletter – the aim being to reach both existing and potential virtual assistants who can become customers.

Before starting to grow her business on Facebook, Jo conducted in-depth research among other Facebook groups and established a set of rules covering both how she would use the platform and the behaviours she expected from members. She is clear on who the group is for, its purpose and how to best manage it (for herself and for the group members). She was determined that it would be a resource to support people who wanted to set up as a VA, and she removes any comments that don't adhere to this. She has set a weekly schedule for posting, including Q&A sessions and wildcard posts to encourage new or shy members to join in. Acknowledging that 95 per cent of her members are parents, she took the decision to freeze the groups over Easter, Christmas and New Year so that everyone could take a well-earned break.

The VA Handbook was one of the first to market in terms of providing online training and a community for virtual assistants. As others have entered the market with competing products and groups Jo has seen little impact in terms of growth. In fact, more conversation about how to become a virtual assistant has potentially increased the discoverability of The VA Handbook via increased search and recommendations.

Analysis

The VA Handbook's success is attributable to research and clarity of purpose. Before setting up the business, Jo established that there was a need for her courses, and she continues to use engagement in the Facebook groups to identify potential new course topics and opportunities to provide useful content. Research and measurement also help her to refine her marketing strategy, by showing her where leads are being generated, and by being ruthless in cutting free from channels that no longer serve her. As she points out, the key is to find out which channel your ideal client favours and post there, rather than broadcasting on every channel.

She is also clear on the purpose of her business and how each channel cross-pollinates the others. This enables her to narrow her focus onto what's working, making efficient use of her time and resources and ensuring that her engagement on her primary platform, Facebook, is done well. As a result of this clarity and authentic approach, her membership is committed to her and the business, and help to maintain the groups as safe spaces for people to encourage and support each other. Group members are loyal advocates and regularly recommend the Facebook groups and products to other virtual assistants.

Resource/CommsHero

www.commshero.com

Background

Founded in 1996, Leeds-based Resource is a marketing services provider that works with the housing, professional services, education, healthcare and automation industries. In 2014, Resource's Sales and Marketing Director, Asif Choudry, questioned why PR and marketing events for his target audience were typically hosted in London, had high ticket costs and were expensive in terms of both accommodation and time. Although the events provided valuable content and networking opportunities, they rarely offered participants a chance to showcase their creativity.

After canvassing a handful of his contacts for their opinion, he decided to put on a value for money event in the north of England (Manchester). It was pitched at a price point that meant his target audience could afford to send their entire team for the cost of sending one delegate to a typical London event. Asif wanted the event to be fun, to celebrate the heroic work done every day by communications professionals, often on declining budgets, and to move away from stale PowerPoint presentations to valuable, interactive learning and tips that could be put into practice immediately.

The first CommsHero event was held in May 2014. Although initially Asif envisaged this as a one-time event, word about it spread and he was invited to organize a similar event in Wrexham (Wales), eventually hosting four CommsHero events in the first year.

Covid-19 lockdowns and restrictions in 2020 and 2021 did not hinder the #CommsHero community. By this time it had become far more than an event. The online conversations continued, and the one-day annual event turned into a week-long virtual event.

Almost ten years later, CommsHero is an annual, week-long hybrid event, with a different theme addressing the hot topics of the day, and attracting top-level speakers including representatives from Greggs, Yorkshire Tea and Innocent.

The CommsHero brand has built momentum through creating a community on social media predominantly X (Twitter). Attendees tweet about their attendance at events and post pictures of themselves holding coveted event 'swag' – physical merchandise such as masks, capes, notebooks and t-shirts – not only during the event but afterwards, with some people posting photos of themselves with the item when they're away on holiday.

The CommsHero campaign has won a number of awards including a CIM Marketing Pioneer Award 2023 for Asif Choudry; and a finalist position at the B2B engage awards in the Best Customer Engagement Initiative and Best Use of Live, Digital and or Hybrid Events Marketing category.

Although CommsHero was established to support and celebrate the work done by Resource's clients and target customers, rather than being an overt pitch for customers (Resource rarely speaks at the events), it has resulted in significant market penetration within their target audiences, requests for pitches and key meetings, and substantial new business has been secured.

Use of social media

Asif had only eight weeks in which to plan the first CommsHero event, but buzz about it grew quickly, solely via social media, creating FOMO (fear of missing out) within the industry. All the event and brand promotion was done on X (Twitter), as that was the platform Asif used personally and which he felt was good for starting conversations. He also felt that X (Twitter) matched the fun personality of the CommsHero brand, whereas at the time, LinkedIn – perhaps a more obvious choice for marketing and PR professionals – was less conversational than it is now.

Asif is active every day on social media, recognizing that it takes time and consistency to build a community. He doesn't schedule tweets but has made it a rule to respond promptly to any post with the hashtag #CommsHero. Thus, anyone in the community who posts about CommsHero is guaranteed a swift reply.

X (Twitter) is used before, during and after events: to create anticipatory buzz, for challenges during the events, and to stay connected and continue conversations after the event.

As part of the ongoing social media content, CommsHero has used X (Twitter) to educate the community on other topics including how everyone can support Muslim colleagues during the holy month of Ramadan. Using the hashtag #CommsHeroRamadan, people are encouraged to give to charity, to fast, spend time in personal or spiritual reflection, or do voluntary work during Ramadan, so that they, too, can feel the physical and spiritual benefits of Ramadan.

Analysis

What is notable about CommsHero's success is the way it blends physical products with social media. Asif has drawn on Resource's design, print and direct mail expertise to create attractive physical products that delegates are delighted to receive, photograph and post on social media. As Asif points out, the impact of direct mail can be difficult to measure, but seeing merchandise on social media enables him to see what's working.

The choice of X (Twitter) as the main platform (though CommsHero now also uses LinkedIn, YouTube and has a podcast) keeps the community in one place and under one hashtag. This creates a sense of belonging and a safe space for the community to share ideas and ask questions, leading to consistent organic growth.

Summary: Seven steps to unlocking social media marketing for business growth

There are a number of corresponding factors illustrated across these success stories and in the examples used throughout this book.

1. **Research**

   All of the success stories highlight the importance of research at every stage of marketing, from establishing there is a customer need to measuring content performance and impacts on lead generation and sales. Ongoing research is essential, because platforms and their features change, clients change how they use each platform and the world around us changes. As we discussed in Chapter 3, it is essential to constantly test and measure and to understand the significance of your business's metrics.

2. **Clarity of purpose**

   Research and measurement should lead to clarity about which products to develop and where to focus efforts for lead generation. As the success stories show, clarity about the purpose of the business and the people it will serve are also key success factors, enabling decision-making and minimizing distractions.

3. **Building authentic brand values**

As discussed in Chapter 4, branding is important to consumers, because identifying with a brand's particular values encourages customers to align themselves with the brand and encourages them to purchase. Partner in Wine, CommsHero and Evoke Classics have clearly defined brand values which both help them to identify the kinds of businesses they want to partner with, and make them visible and unique to potential customers.

4. **Having a face to a brand**

Chapter 5 discussed the importance of storytelling, and all of the success stories have compelling founder stories and people that resonate with followers. Focusing on the personalities behind the brand makes the relationship with the brand more intimate. Followers feel that they know and like the person behind the brand and are invested in their success.

5. **Building a library of content**

Having a social media content calendar is excellent, but you need a regular supply of material to draw on. Routinely filming and photographing behind the scenes, attendance at events or different stages of product development, not only generates authentic, genuine material that resonates with audiences, but also gives a vast repository of material that can be drawn on to fill any gaps in the posting schedule. As we saw in the case study of the VA Handbook, a schedule of evergreen content, regularly updated, is key. For Partner in Wine, video content made a difference to the business overnight.

6. **Having distinct purposes for each social media platform**
   In Chapter 1, we saw how social media has changed consumer behaviour, and also learned how the use of social media itself has evolved, with it now being routinely used as a search engine. Users typically engage with several different platforms, using each one for slightly different purposes. Understanding this enables you to identify a different purpose for each channel, whether that is to educate, to inform, to capture leads, or to direct traffic to your website. As the success stories show, it's not necessary to be on every platform: choosing two and posting regularly can be extremely effective.

7. **Engagement on social media leads to unexpected opportunities**
   Lucy Hitchcock, the founder of Partner in Wine, attributes her products being sold in Selfridges and other high-street stores to her presence on social media. Having an established audience was proof of brand equity. Similarly, Sarah Crabtree's tweet about filming her last series of *Bangers and Cash* led to an unexpected opportunity to work with Evoke Classics on a new venture. CommsHero only intended to create one event for its target audience, but the buzz around it on social media was so great more events were requested and it has grown to an ongoing conversation plus an annual, week-long hybrid event with participants from around the world.

References and further reading

Amazon.com fourth quarter (ended 31 December 2023) results:
https://ir.aboutamazon.com/news-release/news-release-details
/2024/Amazon.com-Announces-Fourth-Quarter-Results/

Kelly-Ann Allen (2021) *The Psychology of Belonging*. Routledge

American Marketing Association: https://www.ama.org/the
-definition-of-marketing-what-is-marketing/

Bain & Company (2024) Global M&A Report: https://www.bain
.com/insights/topics/m-and-a-report/

Rachel Botsman (2018) *Who Can You Trust? How Technology Brought
Us Together – and Why It Could Drive Us Apart*. Penguin.

Robert B. Cialdini (2007) *Influence: The Psychology of Persuasion*.
Harper.

Damian Corbet (2019) *The Social CEO: How Social Media Can Make
You A Stronger Leader*. Bloomsbury Business.

DataReportal: https://datareportal.com/

Facebook unveils Facebook Ads (2007):

https://about.fb.com/news/2007/11/facebook-unveils-facebook
-ads/

Ashley Friedlein, Michelle Goodall (2022) *What is Community Based
Marketing (CBM)? Best Practice Guide*.

https://guild.co/blog/what-is-community-based-marketing/

Nancy Harhut (2022) *Using Behavioural Science in Marketing: Drive
customer action and loyalty by prompting instinctive responses*. Kogan
Page.

Hootsuite (2023) 2023 Social Media Career Report: https://www
.hootsuite.com/en-gb/research/social-media-career-report

Tim Hughes (2022) *Social Selling: Techniques to Influence Buyers and Changemakers.* Kogan Page

Ayelet Israeli, Anne V. Wilson (2023) *Crocs: Using Community-Centric Marketing to Make Ugly Iconic.* Harvard Business School Publishing

Global Trustworthiness Monitor (2023) IPSOS: https://www.ipsos.com/en/trust/trust-social-media

IPA/Brand Finance Investment Analyst Survey (2023): https://ipa.co.uk/news/investment-analyst-survey

Steve Kearns (2021) How to Blend Organic and Paid Media Strategies to Drive More Conversions: https://www.linkedin.com/business/marketing/blog/linkedin-ads/how-to-blend-organic-and-paid-media-strategies-to-drive-more-conversions

Kevin Keller (2019) *Strategic Brand Management: Building, Measuring, and Managing Brand Equity.* Pearson.

The Keller Advisory Group/SUZY Influencer Trust Study. April 2022: https://suzy.com/blog/everyday-influencers-consumers-trust

Khoros (2023) Social media customer service: Importance and stats for 2023: https://khoros.com/blog/social-media-customer-service-stats

Phil Knight, Norbert Leo Butz et al. (2018) *Shoe Dog: A Memoir by the Creator of NIKE.* Simon & Schuster UK.

LinkedIn. 'The Official Guide to Employee Advocacy': https://business.linkedin.com/content/dam/me/business/en-us/elevate/Resources/pdf/official-guide-to-employee-advocacy-ebook.pdf

Scott Magids, Alan Zorfas, Daniel Leemon (2015) The New Science of Customer Emotions. *Harvard Business Review*: https://hbr.org/2015/11/the-new-science-of-customer-emotions

Marriott International (4 April 2023) Marriott International launches new people brand 'Be' to grow and empower global workforce: https://news.marriott.com/news/2023/04/04/marriott

-international-launches-new-people-brand-be-to-grow-and
-empower-global-workforce

Malcolm McDonald and Grant Oliver (2019) *Malcolm McDonald on Value Propositions: How to Develop Them, How to Quantify Them.* Kogan Page

McKinsey & Company (2022) A Better Way to Build a Brand: The Community Flywheel:
https://www.mckinsey.com/capabilities/growth-marketing-and
-sales/our-insights/a-better-way-to-build-a-brand-the-community
-flywheel

McKinsey & Company (2022) Choosing to Grow: The Leader's Blueprint:
https://www.mckinsey.com/capabilities/growth-marketing-and
-sales/our-insights/choosing-to-grow-the-leaders-blueprint

McKinsey & Company (2023) What matters most? Eight priorities for CEOs in 2024: https://www.mckinsey.com/capabilities/strategy-and-corporate-finance/our-insights/what-matters-most
-eight-ceo-priorities-for-2024#/

MBLM (2022) Brand Intimacy Study: https://content.mblm.com/
bis-study-2022-report

Meltwater (2023) Marketing Trends guide: https://www.meltwater
.com/en/resources/marketing-trends

Money.co.uk (2024) UK business statistics and facts 2023:
https://www.money.co.uk/business/business-statistics

Nielsen Content Authenticity Study commissioned by TikTok (2021)
https://www.tiktok.com/business/en-US/blog/nielsen-study-tiktok
-discovery-content-authentic

Marc Randolph (2021) *That Will Never Work: The Birth of Netflix.* Endeavour.

Al Ries and Jack Trout (2001) *Positioning: The Battle for your Mind.* McGraw Hill.

Kevin Roberts (2006) *Lovemarks: The future beyond brands.* powerHouse Books

Signalfire (2020) Creator Economy Market Map: https://www
.signalfire.com/blog/creator-economy

Salesforce (2022) The 8th Edition State of Marketing Report: https://
www.salesforce.com/resources/research-reports/state-of
-marketing/

Salesforce (2023) The 6th Edition State of the Connected Customer:
https://www.salesforce.com/resources/research-reports/state-of
-the-connected-customer/

Mark Schaefer (2023) *Belonging to the Brand: Why Community is the
Last Great Marketing Strategy*. Self-published.

SproutSocial: The Creator Economy: Making Dollars and Sense Out
of Social Partnerships: https://sproutsocial.com/insights/data/
creator-economy/#where-is-the-creator-economy-thriving

Stitch Fix announces first quarter of Fiscal Year 2024 Financial
Results: https://investors.stitchfix.com/static-files/ee09d2b7-6928
-4e99-85e9-7ca64ec89808

Matthew Syed (2021) *Rebel Ideas: The Power of Thinking Differently*.
John Murray.

Unilever (2023) How social media is helping make the switch to
sustainability: https://www.unilever.com/news/news-search
/2023/how-social-media-is-helping-people-make-the-switch-to
-sustainability/

Gary Vaynerchuk, John Hopkinson et al. (2021) *Jab, Jab, Jab, Right
Hook: How to Tell Your Story in a Noisy Social World*. Harper
Business.

Luan Wise (2023) *Planning for Success: A practical guide to setting
and achieving your social media marketing goals*. Independently
published.

Acknowledgements

Writing a book is by no means an isolated project, and it's about far more than the words that go on the page. I'm hugely grateful to all the people I have spoken to – whether it's my industry peers, fellow marketers and business owners, clients and all of those who have attended my training courses and allowed me to test out ideas (sometimes unknowingly) and provide nuggets of insights that I've been able to reflect on. I'm a list writing fanatic, but unfortunately can't name everyone!

My special thanks for contributing to *Smart Social Media* go to those who have supported the proposal and writing process. René Power for every Friday call where we've bounced ideas. Kim Fleet for being there to keep me on track with the right words and flow. Laura Chamberlain for applying your academic rigour (and humour) to my stories.

To those who made time for a coffee conversation to share resources and discuss concepts – Claire Hattrick, Hannah Silverstein and Ruth Dale – thank you. For the quotes and case studies that bring all the words and theory to life – Asif Choudry, Andy Lambert, Damian Corbet, Jo Munro, Leigh Hopwood, Lucy Hitchcock, Lucy Hall, Mike Allton, Noel Anderson, Sarah Crabtree – thank you for sharing your knowledge, insights and experiences with me. Thanks to Amanda Griffiths and Elizabeth

Tindall from Royal Mail MarketReach for sharing case studies that combine traditional media with social media.

To the amazing team at Bloomsbury Business for your hard work and patience. Ian Hallsworth and Allie Collins; it has been great to work on this project with you.

And finally, to the rock that stands beside me in everything I do. The calm behind the scenes. The one who keeps the coffee flowing and my apps up to date. Steven, thank you for being you ♥

About the author

Luan Wise is a chartered marketer and fellow of the Chartered Institute of Marketing (FCIM) with more than 25 years of experience in agency, client-side and consultancy roles. She has worked across a variety of industry sectors, including postal services, manufacturing, recruitment, higher education and professional services – for household names, award-winning institutions and smaller – but perfectly formed – local businesses.

Luan's career in marketing started 'web first', managing content and building online communities. She helped many organizations to produce their first websites. For most of her agency-side career, Luan worked for Hilton, planning and managing complex multimedia, multi-site promotional campaigns for its national and international chain of health clubs. In 2007 Luan switched to become a client-side marketer, joining a start-up business operating in the newly liberalized postal marketplace. With Luan's support, the business won several industry awards and annual sales fast-tracked from £3 million to £60 million within five years.

Seeking a new career challenge, in 2011 Luan started her own marketing consultancy and training business. Since then, she has provided project-based and ongoing support to organizations across the world. She has also delivered numerous industry event talks, group training to thousands of business professionals, plus guest lectures at university business schools.

Luan's expertise in social media was first recognized by LinkedIn as part of its International Women's Day #bestconnected campaign in 2015, which named her one of the top 5 female marketers in the UK. A year later she was signed as a course instructor for LinkedIn's online learning platform. Luan is also an accredited lead trainer for Meta (Facebook and Instagram) and a coach for Google's Digital Garage initiative.

Luan's previous books include *Relax! It's only social media*, *Planning for Success: A practical guide to setting and achieving your social media marketing goals* and *Using Social Media for Work: How to maintain professional etiquette online*.

You can find Luan on LinkedIn, Facebook, Instagram, X (Twitter) and TikTok @luanwise.

Appendix 1: SWOT Analysis

A SWOT analysis is a strategic planning method used to evaluate the Strengths, Weaknesses, Opportunities and Threats involved in a project or in a business venture. It involves specifying the objective of the business venture or project and using primary and secondary research to identify the internal and external factors that are favourable and unfavourable to achieving that objective.

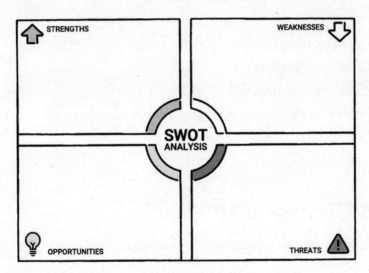

Strengths (Internal)

A business's strengths are its resources, people and capabilities that can be used as a basis for developing a competitive advantage. Examples of such strengths include:

- What you do better than anyone else in your industry
- Strong brand name
- Competitive pricing
- Good reputation among vendors
- Robust cash-flow
- Excellent customer support
- Unique resources

Weaknesses (Internal)

The absence of certain strengths may be viewed as a weakness. For example, any of the following may be considered weaknesses:

- Processes that need improvement
- Losing sales
- A weak brand name
- Poor customer service
- High cost structure
- Not knowledgeable enough about product/service
- Outdated website
- Unique resources

Opportunities (External)

The external environment may reveal certain new opportunities for growth and additional profit. Some examples of such opportunities:

- Arrival of new technologies
- Changes in government regulations
- Unfulfilled customer needs
- Industry trends that you can take advantage of
- A competitor moving or going out of business

- Affiliate/partnering possibilities

Threats (External)

Changes in the external environment may also present threats to the business. Some examples of such threats include:

- Trends that could harm your business
- Shifts in customer needs or tastes away from the firm's products/services
- Competitor activity
- Emergence of substitute products
- New regulations
- Changing technologies

Once you've completed the SWOT analysis, use it to inform strategic decision-making and planning.

Leverage your strengths to capitalize on opportunities, leveraging your core competencies to gain a competitive edge.

Address weaknesses by developing strategies to mitigate or overcome them, whether through training, resource allocation or process improvement initiatives. Similarly, be proactive in addressing threats by implementing contingency plans, diversifying your offerings or strengthening relationships with key stakeholders.

Additionally, use your SWOT analysis to identify strategic priorities and set objectives that align with your findings. Focus on leveraging your strengths to exploit opportunities that offer the greatest potential for growth and profitability, while also addressing weaknesses and mitigating threats to safeguard your business.

Appendix 2: PESTLE Analysis

A PESTLE analysis looks at six key factors – political, economic, social, technological, legal and environmental.

It is a simple listing of bullet points under six key headings that helps examine factors in the wider environment, that can impact a business and your products and/or services.

PESTLE Analysis

P — Political
E — Economic
S — Social
T — Technological
L — Legal
E — Environmental

Below you can find examples of points you might include on your PESTLE analysis.

Political

Government policy, political stability or instability, bureaucracy, corruption, foreign trade policy, tax policy, trade restrictions, labour/environmental/copyright/consumer protection laws, competition regulation, funding grants and initiatives etc.

Economic

Economic trends, growth rates, industry growth, seasonal factors, taxation, inflation, interest rates, international exchange rates, international trade, labour costs, consumer disposable income, unemployment rates, availability of credit, monetary policies, raw material costs etc.

Social

Attitudes and shared beliefs about a range of factors including health, work, leisure, money, customer service, imports, religion, cultural taboos, the environment, population growth and demographics, family size / structure, immigration / emigration, lifestyle trends etc.

Technological

Technology and communications infrastructure, consumer access to technology, emerging technologies, automation, legislation around technology, research and innovation, intellectual property regulation, competitor technology and development, technology incentives etc.

Legal

Laws regarding consumer protection, labour, health and safety, antitrust, intellectual property, data protection, tax and discrimination, international and domestic trade regulations / restrictions, advertising standards, product labelling and safety standards etc.

Environmental

Weather, climate change, carbon footprints, environmental regulations, pollution laws and targets, recycling and waste management policies, endangered species, support for renewable energy etc.

Once you've gathered insights from your PESTLE analysis, use them to inform strategic decision-making and risk management. Identify potential opportunities and threats arising from each factor and develop strategies to capitalize on or mitigate them accordingly. Leverage political stability and favourable economic conditions to expand into new markets or invest in growth initiatives. Adapt to societal changes and technological innovations by updating your products, services or business processes to meet evolving customer needs.

Furthermore, anticipate and navigate regulatory challenges by staying informed about changes in legislation and compliance requirements that may impact your industry.

Appendix 3: Persona Resources

A customer persona, also known as a buyer persona or ideal customer portrait, is a reflection of your ideal target customer based on research and data. It is a detailed profile that includes your customer's demographic information, motivations, preferences and behaviours.

The image below shows what a customer persona template could include.

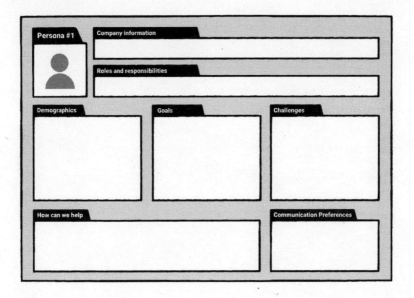

There are several approaches to preparing personas. Starting with industry research and published reports is useful. In the UK, the Office for National Statistics (www.ons.gov.uk) is a good resource for reports related to the economy, population and society at national, regional and local levels. For similar data for non-UK countries, you can find resources via the United Nations statistics division (https://unstats.un.org/home/nso_sites). Industry reports can be found via market research organizations such as Mintel (www.mintel.com).

Combining published research such as Mintel reports with your own business data and research is essential to help you build the best understanding of your target audience. You should consider speaking to existing and prospective customers one-to-one or via focus group interviews.

For more advice, visit the Buyer Persona Institute at www .buyerpersonas.com

Appendix 4: Michael Porter's Generic Strategies

Michael Porter's Generic Strategies framework can be illustrated using a matrix that shows four strategic options based on two key dimensions: competitive advantage and competitive scope. It is illustrated in the image below.

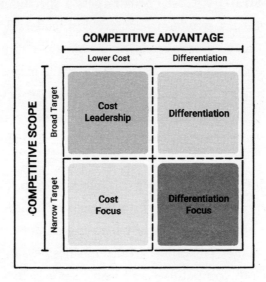

Cost Leadership Strategy: Cost Leadership entails striving to be the lowest-cost producer in the industry while targeting a broad market segment. By offering products or services at lower prices than competitors, businesses can attract price-sensitive customers and gain market share. This strategy requires a relentless focus on operational efficiency, cost reduction and economies of scale to maintain profitability despite lower prices.

Differentiation Strategy: Differentiation involves offering unique products or services with superior quality or innovative features to a broad market segment. This strategy creates perceived value among customers, allowing businesses to command premium prices and build strong brand loyalty. Differentiation requires a deep understanding of customer needs and preferences, as well as continuous investment in product development and marketing to maintain a competitive edge.

Cost Focus Strategy: Cost Focus targets a specific niche market within the industry, striving to achieve cost leadership within that segment. By serving the needs of a smaller, defined customer group, businesses can compete effectively while maintaining lower costs. This strategy involves tailoring products or services to meet the specific requirements of the target market and optimizing operations to minimize expenses while delivering value.

Differentiation Focus Strategy: Differentiation Focus entails offering unique products or services tailored to the needs of a specific niche market segment. By focusing on delivering superior value to a smaller customer group, businesses can differentiate themselves from competitors and foster strong customer loyalty. This strategy requires a deep understanding of the niche market's preferences and demands, as well as a commitment to continuous innovation and personalized customer experiences.

To use the framework, start by evaluating your business's competitive position along the two critical dimensions: competitive advantage and competitive scope. Competitive advantage refers to your ability to outperform rivals either through cost leadership or differentiation, while competitive scope relates to the breadth of your target market, whether broad or focused on a specific niche.

Once you've assessed your current position, you can identify the most suitable strategy based on your strengths, weaknesses and market dynamics. For instance, if you have a strong cost advantage and operate in a broad market, you might pursue a Cost Leadership Strategy to leverage economies of scale and offer products or services at lower prices. Conversely, if you excel in innovation and serve a niche market segment, a Differentiation Focus Strategy may be more fitting to cater to unique customer needs.

The key to effective use of this framework is aligning your chosen strategy with your business's resources, capabilities and market opportunities. You'll need to carefully consider factors like customer preferences, industry dynamics and competitive pressures to ensure your strategy is viable and sustainable in the long term.

Index